SHINE

WHEN CHASING SACRED SPACES GOES DARK

JAMIE WEIL

Library of Congress 2020924119
Library of Congress
US Programs Law and Literature Division
Cataloging in Publication Program
101 Independence Ave., S.E.
Washington, DC 20540-4283

978-1-64184-500-7 | Ebook
978-1-64184-499-4 | Paperback
978-1-64184-504-5 | Hardback

Dedication

For Anthony, here's your book. I'm sorry it's late.

Author's Note

My entire writing career, I have looked toward traditional publishing as the way to go when writing a book. I've done that multiple times. In traditional publishing, as in documentary filmmaking, there is a hierarchical structure that makes for a slow-moving train. At times it can suck the Soul and Spirit out of a work. It's a space where we end up negotiating this and that, each bringing their own unique imprint and filter to that space. When it works well, it's beautiful, and the work is the best it can be. When it doesn't, it's anxiety provoking, exhausting, and slow.

Now is not the time for slow moving trains. It's not a time for hiding. It's a time for power-pivoting and doing things differently and efficiently. This book is my power pivot, and I'm choosing its path because I'm in a hurry to share things with you I know will help you. That's not something I'm willing to negotiate, and that feels exhilarating.

This past weekend, I was talking with my friend, Luna, about signing up for Tom Bird's "Write a Book in a Weekend" retreat, which I've eyed for more than a decade now. I explained I would be taking advantage of the 2020 Lockdown to virtually do the Sedona retreat from the comfort of my red chair, my Lab Kai at my feet. It seemed ideal. Tom has a gift for empowering authors to work as channels for the Divinity that is greater than all of us and simultaneously lives within each of us. The writer becomes the hose, holding space for the flow that gushes through. When I explained the process to my husband, he said, "If you locked me in room and forced me to count words every 15 minutes, that would be like hell." For me, it was the heaven I have always sought in my lifetime as a writer. I will be forever grateful to Tom for opening up this writing third eye and saving me a decade of multiple drafts and loss of my voice to the other. Thank you, Tom, and your team at Sojourn.

As my creation process was so different on this project, Luna asked me how I would publish it. I laughed. "Probably traditionally, but I'm going to ask the book how it wants to see the world."

Luna, a filmmaker who has spent the past 15 years capturing spiritual messages from the world greats in her timely indie documentary *Time of the Sixth Sun*, said, "You're doing this book differently. It needs to come into the world differently."

Luna was right. This is Spirit's book, and Spirit deserves to be fully heard in a timely matter as an offering to you. What you read now, was poured out over the course of the weekend through me but not by me. My fingers typed as I listened for what most needed to be shared right now in this moment, what would most help you to hear. I pray I was a good listener.

A very practical gift came during the second draft in the addition of "light lifts." I have included these at the end of each chapter. Don't skip these! This book is short by intention so you will have some time to sit with it. Have a journal with you as you read. Spend some time with these light lifts and get to know them. They are meant to ignite you with joy. These are daily rituals I use in my own life. You will find your own combo, but these will give you some ideas you may not have tried.

Daily rituals fill our lives. Many are unconscious. Creating a daily light ritual that fits you, your schedule, and your unique vibe, is as crucial to your well-being as daily practices such as brushing your teeth and taking a shower. Think of your daily ritual as an energetic shower. Pick and choose your favorites, add new ones you pick up along the way, and put something into place that will inspire you to do what you came to do.

Be realistic. If you only have five minutes, don't set up a 30-minute routine. After much remolding, I have added to my daily ritual morning energy and grounding practices the following: exercise (30 minutes), meditation (20 minutes), energy cleansing exercises (4 minutes), and time connecting with my husband and dog, first walking, then having coffee (30 minutes.) This starts most of my days. We travel often, so the order is mixed up a bit then, but I aim to always include the first three, even on the road. The idea is not to let your shadow perfectionist archetype take over, but rather to find a ritual that lifts you, that fills you with the light you need to shine. Give yourself grace as you find this balance and start where you are.

One way to keep these in the front of your mind is to put them on your device in a way you will see daily. For example, when I'm starting a new habit or adding a new practice, I will add it to my daily Google calendar, so it pops up on my phone to remind me each day. I also list the top five core values I am holding in focus in my life at the current time. These rotate, depending on where I am in my personal journey. Each day, my calendar pops up my top five and my daily ritual, which will align with those values. Currently, one of those values is spiritual connection so it is essential I don't sidestep my daily meditation, even while I'm on the road or have a big project I'm excited about sinking into from dawn to dusk. That happens to me a lot because I love what I'm doing and when I stop loving it, I pivot. In that process, I try not to sabotage myself, and if I do, I give myself grace to start again. Eventually, the new rhythm sticks. When you find something you love, share it in a way so that others can shine, too. In this way, we all shine.

And for this book to shine required a team effort. Deep thanks to my sons who each helped in their own ways. To Jordan, for your inspiration along the journey and your encouragement to try this a new way. And to Abraham for being my first listener and editor extraordinaire, thank you for hearing and seeing *Shine*. To my mom, for your lightning speed editing. Your turnaround time is unprecedented. To Haumea for clearing the way for me to end my writer's strike, and to Luna for the encouragement I needed to power-pivot and take ownership of my own intuitive creativity journey. Finally, to Ellie and Aubrie, thank you for sharing your stories with me and with the world. Keep shining, for as you shine, the world shines. I love you all to the bottom of the sea and beyond.

Table of Contents

Prologue

As I rewrote the first draft of this book, it became clear what it wanted to be. First and foremost, it wanted to be stories that would get you quickly to peace, happiness, and trauma recovery from a world that turned topsy-turvy there for a minute. It wanted to be a healing balm, one with practical tools you could use in triage fashion as a tourniquet to stop the hemorrhaging. It wanted to feel easily approachable, even to those who don't like to read, or who often find themselves listening to audio books (hand raised!) just because it's hard to sit still at times. It wanted to do all that on a plane ride from the West Coast to Hawaii where I read many of my books, and it wanted to be infused with the talk-story vibe and spirit of Big Island aloha. It wanted to make you shine as brightly as you are meant to shine. It wanted to remind me to do the same.

It's easy to lose ourselves, or in many cases, to still be seeking who we are at our core well beyond the Second Act of our lives. The search can be daunting. If someone put me in an empty house alone and told me I could create the space just how I wanted, I think I would sit and stare at that blank canvas for some time before I could make the space truly me. I would need that time to get to the core of my deepest self. In truth, I'm not sure I've ever really been there. I struggle with knowing where I begin and where others' influence over me stops. I am a daughter, a wife, a mother, a friend, a mentor, a mentee, a teacher, a student, a writer, a reader, and a gazillion other things. During my entire life one or more of those relationships have required that I collaborate, negotiate, compromise, and dim down a part of my light in order to create the peace, harmony, and joy I strive to have in my life. They've also made me shine. While I deeply love all those roles I named, and define myself so much by them, I struggle to identify who exactly I am without all the whisperings of other in my ear, the sacrifices I have made for the sake of that other and they for me. The Covid has magnified this question. This is what I mean when I say I write this book as much for me as for the world.

I certainly do not have everything figured out or think I am an authority of any kind in this space. Instead, these stories are an offering to an interconnected world moving through unprecedented times. My deepest hope is that this book can bring light and sunshine into each Soul with a knowing that when each of us shines, the whole world shines brighter.

As I revised, I held my most special people in front of me and looked for words I would offer them to reconnect with the sparks of light I see so brightly when I look at their hearts. I started with my own sons, both of whom helped teach me these tools in their own unique and magnificent ways. I owe each of them infinite gratitude for their contributions to this book and to me as a Soul. I worked my way through my innermost circle out to all the others yet to be discovered – in my heart, imagining an understanding and embracing of what I know to be true: we are all connected and capable of the deepest love and kindness. I imagined a world where it is far easier to love than hate, for the moment we spend energy on hate, we dim down our own light and make the world heavier. Now is the time we must choose which role to play in the world, and we can't afford "heavier."

I didn't want to just offer another self-help recipe book filled with magical thinking and sage. Instead, I wanted to quickly offer a starting point of reconnection with that unique and beautiful part that longs to be recognized by you. To do that, I needed to be willing to be fully me, something I have steered away from most of my life for fear of being driven into the ditch of judgment, rejection, abandonment – all those deep-seated fears that emanate from each of us. Here's the irony. Until we are ready to drop the façade of who we think others should see, we are much more powerless to all those things we fear. We hide behind our influences of tribe – of family, religion, politics, friends, and community. These influences will bully us to remain in status quo. If Covid has taught us anything, it's that status quo stinks.

Instead, love more, and fear less. Don't be afraid to hug. Don't be afraid to use the word love in all its glorious contexts. These words apply first to that part inside of you that has not been loved as you needed, and next to everyone who shares our world. In this way, in this full loving acceptance of who you really are and came to be, you will not only shine the brightest light you can shine, you will light up the whole freaking world around you.

CHAPTER ONE:

Seeing Your Beauty

You can't change the way the wind blows,
but you can adjust your sails.

—Anonymous

When I met Anthony, he was 17 and full of life. He met my husband and me in a café in sunny Laguna Beach, California, and could hardly wait to take my youngest son with him around the beauty that the stunning California Coast has to offer.

The ocean was Anthony's first love. The way the white waves crashed into the high, rocky cliffs made his eyes beam. The way the cerulean waters sparkled in the sunshine drew him toward it. The committed way the waves crashed into the shore over and over again offered the dependability he struggled to find in his life. Anthony carried that ocean glimmer in his Soul. When he talked about the sea, his eyes flashed like sun diamonds dancing on the water.

He wanted to take Jordan on an adventure that day, chasing sacred space. We weren't sure exactly what that meant, but at the end of the day, we could tell they found it, exploring cliff houses under construction, beaches with the breeze blowing just right, an Uber bill that would blow your mind. The pictures Anthony took that day showed how he saw the world, how he saw this space between land and sea, and how he wanted to share it. The shots he took of Jordan, also a lover of the sea, warm my heart to this day. Anthony captured Jordan's Soul, and when someone sees the beauty of your child's Soul the way you see it, you can't help but love that person deeply.

Jordan went off to college and Anthony ended up leaving Laguna Beach, moving away from his first ocean love. Several years later, I ran into him in a store far from the ocean in Northern California, where he was selling shoes. We hugged and talked about going to lunch. The sparkle that came with the ocean had left him. I could feel that. On Mother's Day that year, he wrote me a note. He told me I was a good mother, that I should know that, and that he really wanted to read my book *First Break*, my first young adult novel about a protagonist in the throes of a psychotic break who also found peace in the sea. I told him I would buy him lunch, and I would bring him a signed copy.

Things got busy. I was in the middle of making a docuseries on youth mental illness that I was extremely passionate about getting quickly to a world of teens I felt were being ignored and hurting. Teens like Anthony. Days piled on days until months had gone by and I heard rumors Anthony had turned to substances to cope with his sadness. Meanwhile, Jordan went off to study in Italy and they lost communication. In early November, Jordan sent a message from Milan with a screen capture of a social media exchange: *Anthony is dead?*

I went down the social-media rabbit hole and found Anthony's last post, which came on Halloween night. It was a meme of The Joker with the words, "As soon as I tried to get help with my mental health, they tell me to come back in two months." The picture shows The Joker going into an emergency room, being turned away, then getting hit by a car. As I read through the thread of traumatized teens, I felt my heart drop to the bottom of the ocean.

Sadness and regret pushed my face in the sand until I nearly suffocated. My son, oceans away, would not be able to properly say goodbye. I had not made good on our lunch plan and taken Anthony my novel. A beautiful life lost. I wrote a blog that day that would be my last one for quite some time, words to honor sweet Anthony and all the Anthonys of the world: Souls that so clearly had a light sparkling, Souls that lit up in those sacred spaces they loved, Souls I wanted to see shine. Now, I return to this writing space to contemplate this question: what is sacred space? What do we think of when we hear those words? Are they spaces we chase, and in the chasing, miss them entirely?

There are those sacred spaces that are related to historical or spiritual links. We think of Machu Picchu with its journey up many stairs. We think about Camino de Santiago, the long walk people take to get more clarity on who they are in this world and space. We think about Sedona's Boynton Canyon where Cucina Wo/Man sits, morphing with the time to hold simultaneous space for both Divine Feminine and Divine Masculine. We think of Mount Shasta in California's North, a magical mountain to which people are called from all over the world to come and live near. In fact, a poll of Mt. Shasta's residents will have many saying, "The Mountain just called, and I ended up here. It's the weirdest story." We think of the Big Island of Hawaii with its incredible Kealakekua Bay where bones of royalty sleep in the steep cliffs that hug the bay and create a space for the best snorkeling on the island. Mauna Kea, on that same island, has long been a battleground between the sacred and science. Science fights for more observatories, while the native Hawaiians fight for their sacred space to practice ritual and connect with Spirit. And we can't mention sacred space without thinking about Jerusalem where so many faith paths intersect, and so much conflict floods that intersection.

Sacred spaces, then, can be places defined by all these different bits of land where others have swarmed, where many have found stories that help them understand themselves better, and where there is often conflict at one time or another. Or, in Anthony's case, it can simply be a place in nature, an ocean so large and powerful that meets the sand over and over, a reliable friend. It can be a forest, a rose garden, or a Kama Sutra moment between lovers where everything else falls away, just for that moment.

The important piece: each person must learn where to find their own sacred space. Each of us has a sense of where ours is when we arrive on this planet. For Anthony, it was the ocean, but he fell away and couldn't find his way back in time. We must do everything we can to build and claim our sacred space. This must remain a priority.

This isn't optional. It's mandatory. Each person has a sacred space and it is each of our responsibilities to figure out where ours is for the sake of our own peace, as well as the peace of the world. Only when we figure out where this space is within our own Soul and psyche will we find the peace we seek. Only when we figure out where our sacred space is, will we figure out how to charge ourselves up with the power we need to get where we're meant to go. Each person comes to this planet with a direction, a secret treasure map dictated by their own desires and sensibilities, and on some level we all know intuitively what that is. But life is the great distractor, and we are taught by our cultures, by our family of origin, by our social constructs of religion, political tribes, and educational institutions what to believe, what will make us full and happy, charged-up to travel more miles. Only when we get going, sometimes well on down the road, do we realize we left the charging station too early.

Where is your sacred space? Is it in your own backyard? Is it in someone else's? Is it in nature? In a bustling city? Is it in a habit, or substance, or quick fix that doesn't serve you? Where is the place you feel most at peace? Figuring this out is not an extracurricular activity. It's mandatory. The importance of asking yourself this question, and answering it, is truly a matter of life and death for living your Soul's purpose.

Not asking the question brings you to a place you've always been. Research has shown that 90% of each day is a result of early programming that is so unconscious, you don't even know why you do what you do. You go to sleep on the same side of the bed every night. You get up. You go to the bathroom. You follow more or less the pattern from the day before. That entire 90%, directed by subconscious programing from the first six years of childhood, dictates the day, the week, the month, the year. The 10% of space that is conscious can help you create a container for the other 90% and understand why you do what you do. As you begin to see – and you will with focus, intention, and practice – you will begin to understand not only why it's important to identify your sacred space, but also why it's so important to tap into it.

Where to start? Think about your earliest memory of being really happy. For me, that's the water. My earliest memory, when I was still in diapers, is knocking down all the magazines off a bookshelf into a huge "swimming pool" and pretending to swim in them. My next memory is filling an old huge tire with a tarp over it with water and making a pool for my friend Laurie and me to play in during the hot Northern California summers. Finally, from about two years old on, I could be found underwater from early morning to late night in the above-ground pool in my backyard building mermaid caves with floats. My sacred space? The water, specifically the ocean, and even more specifically, underneath the water in the ocean. It's where I am most me and if it's been too long since I've been there, I need to recreate it. I keep Dr. Teale's bath salts in business with the multiple bags of Epsom salts I pour in my bath to make my own ocean when I can't get to one.

What is your earliest memory of feeling happy? Identify that. Write about it. Spend time with it. Embrace it. Who were you with? Where were you? Identifying this unique truth can be the first step to uncovering your sacred space.

Light Lift 1: Root Yourself Here

Stand, preferably with bare feet on the grass, with your feet shoulder width apart, hands at your side with fingers spread and facing the same way you are facing. Close your eyes. Breathe in deeply through your nose and fill your belly with that air. As you exhale, imagine a strong trunk dropping down through the center of your body and sinking all the way to the core of the earth. Feel the strength of this pull to the earth. You have come to this planet for a specific reason and feeling the connection between your feet and this central trunk dropping down through your center is a great way to remember that. Let the earth support you. Grounding yourself in this way doesn't take long and can make a huge difference in the way your day rolls out.

CHAPTER TWO:

The Covid as Teacher

The moment we cease to hold each other, the sea engulfs us, and the light goes out.

—James Baldwin

When The Covid hit, I was slammed with the same feeling I had when Anthony left. (I call it The Covid because it became this huge beast we all created together, like The Market.) This feeling is one of being overtaken by something so gigantic and powerful that we collectively have our faces pushed into the sand until we can't breathe. Words are so hard to find, especially at first before sorting out the feelings. I watched as people struggled alongside me. I wanted to help, but it was as if we were all in an ocean treading water and a huge tsunami was approaching. The best way for each to help the whole was to help themselves.

As the days rolled into weeks, and I had more time than usual to go within, the words started showing themselves one by one. My heart started opening wider than before. I could look around at others treading, and not just focus on keeping myself above water. The same dynamic was happening with others, as if our newborn eyes were seeing our connection for the first time. I needed to create, to channel this emotion into projects that would give both myself and others emotional buoyancy. I gathered a few friends and creatives with similar hearts, to imagine a way we, as filmmakers, could use talents in a new way. Originally, we had planned to be out on a shoot, capturing a story we were excited about sharing, but along with the rest of the film industry, we were halted from shooting in the traditional ways for some time. We brainstormed how we could power-pivot, a word I would hear many times over the next few months. We figured out a way to tell Kassandra's story. Kassandra was a 19-year-old university freshman with aspirations to be an immigration lawyer. She had shared what growing up Latina in a border town felt like and revealed what navigating bipolar illness was like for her in that container. We were generated, inspired, and excited by the power-pivot.

About a week later, proving the collective was looking around to see how it could gather to co-create, I answered a call for a group project to tell a story of BOTH sides of The Covid, a story we were not seeing mainstream media tell. In the first Zoom call, I noticed my intuition had guided me to something magical. With deep gratitude, I joined a group of 257 filmmakers to bring creatives from all across the world to tell a story of hope, #ChooseHopeStory. We navigated time zones, had early-morning virtual dance parties, nightly meetings, and 10,000 messages on Slack, a project management platform for such things I later bought stock in. I met Kristian, a filmmaker from Chicago, who would become such a teacher for me during this time. In teams, we talked about all the sides of The Covid, how it was hitting us personally, how it was affecting the world, and the images we could bring to the world to lift that up without denying what was happening. We accomplished that feat, chasing some semblance of hope together, and miraculously, we did this in 10 days and released it to the world. This chasing of hope, this sacred container which we created, inspired us all. One month later our Kassandra team told the story of Ellie, an emerging artist also struggling with bipolar illness. We called this series *Social Distancing Together – for the health of it* and put it on Instagram TV for the world to see for free.

Stories: this is how we understand the world, says Joseph Campbell. A favored professor at Sarah Lawrence College, and former Hawaii resident, Campbell taught his students beyond all else to follow their bliss. If I were to point to another sacred space, it would be Campbell's archives of work looking at world religions and myths, housed by Pacifica University in Southern California. Indeed, I found myself there with this angel of a man, the overseer of Campbell's body of work, who may have been an even more dedicated Campbell groupie than I. When I pulled one of the huge books from Campbell's collection, I think myths from Antarctica or some place with lots of snow, I saw these sentences underlined with a ruler and some pristine notes. I remembered the words that Campbell had told his students at Sarah Lawrence College when they asked him what his bliss was. "Underlining sentences," he'd said. I saw that in the linear ink, in the precise shape of the tiny letters that hailed from his generation. I felt his joy of discovering threads that run through all the stories across time. That discovery was his sacred space. That was his bliss.

When The Covid hit, we were all invited to approach sacred space in a new way because we were not able to find it in the ways we had before. We could no longer just hop on a plane and fly to Peru. We weren't allowed. Our regular bliss portals closed up. Robert Ohotto, an intuitive and astrologer on the cutting edge of all things, calls The Covid our "World's First Synchronicity," which I love because I'm a synchronicity junkie. A term originally introduced by Carl Jung (1875-1961) *synchronicity* describes two things that happen "coincidentally" but don't seem to have a logical connection. For example, you are thinking about your mom and she calls right then. Synchronicity. You are thinking about a blue butterfly and one lands on your hand. Synchronicity. Why are these signs, these connections, important to recognize? These are the breadcrumbs to your purpose on this planet. When you pay attention to these, you get more, and the more you pay attention, the more you get. Beyond being feel-good winks from the Universe to let you know you're on the right path, synchronicities can fuel a deep connection with that which is bigger than you. Being mindful of this guidance is one of the easy secrets to a joyful life.

We want to align with our Soul purpose on this planet, because when we do, life flows and is much more fun. Simple, really. It's not *just* that, but it's also that fun powers us up with joy and lifts the planet in such a significant way that we all benefit. If The Covid, which some (not the news, but the metaphysical types) call a sacred invitation, teaches us anything, it's how connected we are to all beings and happenings in our Universe.

Just before The Covid hit, I was in one of those sacred spaces in Sedona, Arizona, called Boynton Canyon. Steep red rocks with ancient dwellings still intact in the cliffs, and a canyon that feels like a giant hug, Boynton Canyon houses one of the top spa resorts in the world. Still, in this space, which is pretty much perfection, stress lives on people's faces, in their tones, in their impatience to get what they need to find peace. The Hurry Up and Relax Syndrome. As The Covid spread its tentacles through the world, and the world prepared for a time out, the resort got emptier and emptier until the last day my husband and I were about the only ones left. It was both lovely and lonely. Lovely, because we got so much extra attention we don't usually get because of the crowds. I swam alone in the pool in the rain. Pure magic. Lonely, because I wanted the world to experience how amazing this space was when it was allowed to be quiet. I knew people needed this peace, especially now.

As we made our way home, I wondered how the world would change. I wondered how we would change. Would we get to the "we" or fight for the "me?" As words like *lockdown* were introduced and *panic buying* became a thing, we saw it would be a split between both. Much like the early stages of the psychotic break that Anthony most likely experienced that dismal October, the world had transformed to a place where isolation, lack of abundance, mask power struggles, and a variety of different approaches to the whole thing, would become the norm, all of it driven by fear.

In contrast to this shutting down, an opening started to happen. Opportunities that had never been so generously offered, presented themselves. Zoom became a household name, shortly followed by Zoom bombers. I made a decision I would come out on the other side of lockdown a kinder, compassionate, smarter, more creative, person. I could see others doing this, too. Everyone's unique print became magnified under these unprecedented times. Curiosity and learning rushed to the fore of my every move, the choices I'd make. Classes I'd heard about for years suddenly became attainable. Dr. Laurie Santos, a professor at Yale University, teaches *Principles of Well Being*, which she created after a concern about seeing so many college students with anxiety, depression, and a clear scale of mental illnesses rising. She wanted to discover what the science behind happiness really is. She designed this class, consistently one of the most popular at Yale, and when The Covid came to call, Santos and Yale offered the course free to anyone who wanted to take it. My cohort at last check was 1,800,000 strong, though nearly everyone I knew that started with me dropped out – though I won't name names.

That class reminds us of what we already know, but it also tells us that knowing is not enough. That's called the GI Joe fallacy, by the way, to think that knowing is most of the battle. Science shows that it is the practices part that brings the happiness home, not the knowing. In that regard, the class comes with an app called *ReWi*, a black-and-white icon of a brain, which breaks down into eight categories what we should be doing each day. Here they are: meditation, exercise, sleep (seven-eight hours), kindness, connection, savoring, gratitude, goal setting.

The reason we hit each of these each day is simply for our own happiness and the science behind doing this is abundant.

These are not the categories, at least in the United States, we have been taught to chase. In the U.S., we have been taught to chase the house, the car, the high-paying job, the relationship with someone who is our person. We are taught this by the constructs of our society and those lessons are reinforced by the social-media messages that bombard us. The advertisers and media play into these mind-melds and these become what we teach our kids from the time they are babies; we are trying to get them on the prestigious preschool lists before they are even born.

Before I became a teacher, I was one of those difficult parents, the ones teachers dread and talk about in the teacher's lounge. I didn't mean to be, but I was under extreme stress. A single parent working in a high-pressure dysfunctional job, my first child's teachers were in my target zone of that stress and when I interacted with them, I was not even close to my best. Years later when I became a teacher with my own classroom of students and endless duties, I suddenly understood what they were going through.

One of those pressures is to address the issue of early signs of mental illness in the classroom. Over the past decade, the increase in students showing symptoms has skyrocketed and, paired with a lack of support for educational leaders at least in my country, we have an epidemic on our hands. In conversations with teachers across the U.S., in both rural and urban areas, I hear clear frustration about lack of resources and knowledge of how to help these struggling young people when it counts. As a teacher myself in the early '90s, I received a Masters' in Teaching from a great college, though I had no instruction on helping my students who were showing early symptoms of mental illness. The biggest price is that when we don't address this issue early, we set our children up for a dismal future, which is so much harder to fix after the fact. The child suffers deeply, misses out on their childhood, struggles with relationships with others and themselves, and at times ends up completing suicide. (Suicide awareness communities call it *completing suicide* vs. *committing suicide* because one *commits* a crime.)

For a peek into this world, meet Aubrie. I met her after beta testing the pilot of a docuseries on youth mental illness in her eighth-grade classroom. She came up to me and identified herself as a writer and offered to share some of her writings. Having lived a fairly traumatic first 12 years of her life, she had turned to writing as her sacred space, the space that literally saved her life throughout multiple suicide attempts. This poem, written when Aubrie had barely turned 14, was a suicide note she had written. It emanated from a song she could not get out of her head, a song called *Tear Myself Apart* by Tate McRae. Reacting to the repeat in her brain, she wrote this.

and so it goes
by Aubrie

and so it goes
no one knows
what's in our pretty heads
the thoughts that race as we go to bed
and the way we feel, never felt so real
the love we give, the hate we receive,
the perfect smiles on our faces too easily deceive
the tears that fall, we're on the run
from what we fear, and everyone
because what's done is done
our reflection shows what no one knows
that we're broken, defeated, and all alone
the reflections show what we aim to deceive
that all is well and we have everything we need
and when the reflection falters
no matter who hollers
we can no longer hear
because of the fact
that the end is near

one last time we're on the run
due to the statement, what's done is done
two words, i'm sorry
for never being good enough
for not fighting when the tides were tough
so when the sun sets
and the night falls
i'll become a star in the sky
leaving everyone to wonder why
and love we'll meet again
but for now, watch the sky as days go by
i promise love that i will be waiting on the other side
and so it goes
you didn't know
and i'm so sorry, but it's my time to go.

Aubrie is one of the most prolific, gifted writers I know and is still in her early teens. A month ago, she sent me a note, having stayed up all night to read my second young adult novel, *Intuition*. It was one of those notes you receive that makes you deeply happy you followed your dream to become a writer because it inspires others, like Aubrie, to follow their dream to become a writer. It had also nudged her back to her sacred space. Reading my novel had inspired her to pull out pen and paper, take the toxicity that fills her current story, and channel it into her story. Writing is her sacred space and there is no doubt, that as she holds to this space, she will gift the world with genius.

We learn as we go, so we must stay and hold to that. The lessons we are taught, both inspiring and violating, are the ones we learn through our connections with others. We frame our values around what we learn in these interactions. At some point, we may realize the ladder was up against the wrong wall. We climbed up that ladder with the promise from our parents, teachers, and those we believed, only to find that what we really wanted, needed, was on the other building.

I think of Jim Carrey's story, and Tom Shadyac, the film-maker who discovered him. Both lived in Los Angeles where practically everyone is either in The Business, working on being in The Business, or dodging it all together. As an Angeleno for 30 years, I was in the last category and ironically had no interest in using film to tell stories until returning to my small hometown in Northern California. Carrey went the other way. The story is often told of how he used visualization with the idea of "if you dream it, you can make it happen." He did this with money. If Hollywood legend is to be believed, he drove to the top of Mulholland Drive and looked out over the city seeing himself as a prominent actor and wrote out a check to his name as payment for those services. He quickly achieved his goal. However, once he did, years later he realized that wasn't the goal that brought him happiness, and he went on to do community service with troubled teens in downtown LA. He also found a sacred space in creating artwork and has become a prolific painter.

When Tom Shadyac discovered Carrey, all the riches that he had been told would make him happy followed: the palatial Pasadena estate, the private jet, the Hollywood trappings to which many aspire. Yet, as he recounts in one of my favorite documentaries *I Am*, when he stood looking at all his material success in his Pasadena foyer, he still felt unhappy. It was an accident on a mountain bike that hit him upside the head (literally) causing a severe concussion followed by a dark depression. Following his dark night of the soul, he gathered a crew to figure out what was wrong with the world and ended up discovering what was right. He sold much of his stuff, moved into a trailer park in Malibu, and rode his bike to Pepperdine University, where he taught in the Communications Department sharing his story of Love and collaboration with the students.

The cycle that Carrey and Shadyac went through resulted from being taught that certain things will bring us happiness. We chase those. We measure ourselves against that worth, locked in situations and relationships that do not serve our highest good, only to find out in the end, our true sacred space is some place quite different from where we are.

Where is your sacred space? Where do you feel most present? When was the last time you looked around at all corners of the moment and felt its perfection? Are you chasing goals you have thought were your own but are really influenced by others around you? When was the last time you were deeply inspired? What inspires you? Give yourself grace, and the gift of honesty. Pretend you are interviewing your best friend and treat yourself accordingly. Answer those questions as if your life (and our world) depends on it.

Light Lift 2: Gifting Yourself the Present

Sit or stand, feet flat on the floor, spine erect. Close your eyes. Inhale through your nose and slowly count to 7. Fill up your belly and make sure your chest is not rising. This helps you breathe deeply and immediately brings you into the present moment. Hold your breath in your belly for 7 counts. Slowly exhale through your nose for 7 counts. At the end of the exhale, when all the air has left your lungs, pause for 7 counts before taking your next breath. Repeat the cycle 5 times. This also works great before public speaking or an awkward conversation. Simple, free, and always available, deep breathing in your ritual will train your body to automatically do this when under stress instead of holding its breath.

CHAPTER THREE:

The Hamster Wheel

There's more to life than making it go faster.

—Dr. Wayne Dyer

When my family lived in the city, it seemed like it was always in motion. We were tucked away in a gated community with a lovely waterfall that cascaded down a back hillside through a garden paradise we had created. We could block out the noise and the fact that our neighbors lived fewer than 20 feet away from where we slept. We lived near a hospital, the one where I had both our babies, so ambulance noise was fairly common and sent a surge through me every time I heard it. Though Target was only eight miles from our home in Southern California's South Bay, it could take up to 30 minutes to get there in traffic, and it always seemed like there was traffic. The psychic noise blared constantly.

When we moved to the country 12 years ago, it was a return for me back to the small ranch town in Northern California where I grew up. Here, everyone sits on 3.5-acre lots with plenty of room between. Many of the people who live here have always lived here and not much changes, which is how they like it. The quiet at dusk and dawn is pierced by the deafening sound of crickets and a huge variety of birds, including regular geese who fly over our back yard announcing their presence. Traffic isn't a thing, except the rare occasion when roadwork is happening; then the whole town discusses the "traffic" situation. The psychic space is notably wide, and we definitely feel like we breathe deeper when we compare the two ways of being on the planet.

This isn't to glamorize it. My town has a sign that says "No Room for Racism" which wouldn't be a problem except there's a bullet hole through it that has been there for decades. With generational lack of education often comes poverty, fear-based thinking, and small-mindedness formed by tribe. It doesn't touch everyone in small towns, but it definitely touches many.

When I return to various cities, which I do often for both work and play, I notice differences right away. First, not everybody smiles and waves, which is mostly what happens where we live. It's one of the things I love. Second, the city stress level is palpable, as people try to get from one place to another blaring their horns at each other, cutting off other drivers in traffic, standing in long lines for everything from coffee to car washes. When I visit friends in cities and homeless people ask for money, my friends seem so numb to the repetitive asking, it seems they barely recognize this is another human being in desperate need. In the city, there is much to do, and a gazillion people trying to do it. Every time we go, I need to learn new systems for getting around, parking, and getting anywhere on time because it's always changing. And yet, what the city has to offer is delicious: its culture, diversity, restaurants, museums, spas, resorts, and entertainment venues hold me close. I love them all.

When we are in constant motion like this, and sometimes this is necessary to survive, we pay a cost that is not so apparent.

In fact, moving all the time is the ego setting up a defense mechanism to protect itself. For a hamster on a hamster wheel, all it knows is it needs to keep moving because that's how it's always been. When we are taught by the hamsters we are around that this is what we should do, we imitate. It's automatic. Sometimes we don't even understand why we need to keep moving. And if someone reaches in and stops it, we don't know what to do with ourselves.

How, then, if we are so indoctrinated by being in constant motion, by distracting ourselves by going here and there, can we find the place that is sacred, the space we are looking for? How do we do that? This is the scenario the world found itself in following the 2020 Lockdown. The Covid reached in and grabbed the wheel. Everyone scrambled and fell off the wheel. Many called it a pandemic, a horrible thing. Others called it a sacred gift, an opportunity to reset, a call to unity. Some developed symptoms of mental illness; mental illness rates rose globally. Some found a power-pivot and moved into high creative gear. Almost everyone, with the exception of the new "essential workers classification," lost their jobs or started working at home. Based on the daily trending of the #writers on Twitter, I'm willing to hypothesize that many decided to write their book, that story inside them that always wanted to come out but never had the time to materialize. One thing was certain: we had new, unprecedented ways to chase sacred space.

Sacred spaces: even if we get them right, can they be found by chasing? As The Covid morphed into Covid Season with no end in sight, we watched the changes around the world like some grand, anthropological study. In California, all beaches and parks were closed and in areas like Los Angeles, going outside without a mask was a ticketed offense. In more rural areas, there were different rules early in the season and soon the mask would become a way people would exert their power and powerlessness, quickly politicizing what it meant to be masked. Interestingly, though, as the to-mask-or-not-to-mask war raged on, we as both individuals and a collective were being called to show our unique selves that we'd been hiding, to open our hearts to who we really are as a true remedy to help ourselves and everyone else.

Writing this book was that for me. I've always tried to fit in because I felt so different here on this planet. I write children's literature because I loved both reading it to my own children, and teaching it to my students. I figured that I'd spent so many hours taking from the body of work, I needed to give back. The same came with film. I'd been a fervent movie-watcher since my early teens, going to work in a movie theater at 16, and staying until 3:00 a.m. with the crew to keep current on the latest films. One of my young memorable birthday presents was when a guy I was dating surprise-arranged a sneak preview in this beautiful, old Westwood theater he managed during college. He arranged a viewing of *Chances Are,* a reincarnation movie starring Cybil Shepherd, that hadn't been released yet and that he knew I was so excited to see. On my birthday morning, a blindfold came out, and after a mysterious drive, I walked into a dimly lit cathedral filled with flowers, Cinnamon Toast Crunch, and warm cinnamon rolls which we devoured as we watched the movie alone in this huge theater. Magical. After many experiences with film, I finally decided I needed to give back to this medium in which I had taken pleasure for so long.

In both cases, I was responding to a type of prompting, but not the deeply spiritual part of myself that I had grown up hiding in my Southern Baptist town. It didn't feel safe to be who I truly was. I didn't feel safe to share what I knew were my core gifts. I began having this conversation with other people during Covid Season who were feeling the same way. It was as if being locked down, and taken off the hamster wheel, had opened a portal for self-exploration of the deepest kind, one where we would need to sit with our issues of power and powerlessness, and one where we would be invited to go within, distraction free, and find our true selves. The beauty here is there is a new quiet, with Ram Dass from the beyond whispering, "Enjoy."

If we can talk ourselves into getting off the hamster wheel, we've won. The ego, though, doesn't want that. It wants to be busy and be seen. It wants to get things done and figure out how we can jump into drama. For those in the world who are highly sensitive people, terms like empaths or empathic souls are ones to study. Empaths/empathic souls feel both their own energy and the impact of the collective energy, intensely. Empaths are wired differently and experience life beyond the five-sensory model. The empath dances in a multisensory space with the music cranked up louder than others perceive.

How do you know you are an empathic soul? Like me, perhaps you feel like your family members see you as "different." You are highly sensitive in all ways and know things you aren't always sure how you know. Busy sensory spaces like amusement parks can drain you, especially if you have not learned how to protect yourself when you are in them. You absorb energy and need to learn ways to alchemize it instead. You are a light worker. We are all psychic, but you have the deepest level of knowing, are often dismissed by others, and this causes you to mistrust yourself. Others do that because of your light, which they feel they must dim down. They feel they must dim you down because if you shine, you may expose shadows they are afraid to show.

Much addiction comes from this space. When humans who feel at multisensory levels step into this 5-sensory world, it's overwhelming. Everything is much louder. Usually around middle school, when hormones bring on an added level of noise, one way teens deal with this noise is to begin experimenting with substances (food, drugs, alcohol, sex, self-injury) to turn down the volume and numb out. Those strategies can quickly morph into addictions (and/or psychotic breaks) for highly sensitive souls in a world that has not yet figured out the importance of these souls to the future of our world. What's more, a huge increase of empaths/empathic souls are appearing on the planet with no strong support system in place. They will shift this dynamic simply by being here, but often at their own cost and painful journey.

Both Dr. Judith Orloff and Robert Ohotto have their own prescriptive ways to teach to this topic. If you are an empath/empathic soul, it's imperative you educate yourself about this topic. It's important to find the personal pathways that work best for you in unique times of herd feeling and collective thought. These powerful thoughtforms impact empaths even more strongly, often before they even realize what's happening. For example, many empaths, including me, unexplainably started feeling depressed last December. The same thing is happening as I type this, and Michelle Obama has recently revealed her "low grade" depression. It's important to learn your own system and distinguish between what is yours and what you are picking up from the collective energy. It makes sense that you will have both. We are all connected. One energy. This is the idea of holism and Covid Season repeats this theme in its new marketing campaigns and strategies. We are moving to *we* – and it's a good thing.

It's really a matter of being awake. Right now, in this incredible time, more people are waking up than ever before. There are many different pathways, but the overall gestalt is that eyes are opening, hearts are opening, and people are becoming conscious of the truth that we are all connected, and that what happens to one, happens to all. The Covid has taught us this lesson. In each of us, then, as we join our fellow humans in this truly sacred space, our role becomes to keep ourselves the healthiest balance we can in all our bodies: physical, mental, emotional, and spiritual.

Feeling is such a part of being alive. We want to feel. It's why we love stories. We remember so much more from stories than from statistics. Stories make us feel. They're why people are drawn to religion with its beautiful stories and ways of understanding how to be in the world. I have never been great at being religious, but I find such beauty, like Joseph Campbell did, in the themes that run through all the world's religion. Like love. Like kindness. Like compassion. The golden threads.

Ask yourself this: am I an empath/empathic soul? Whether you are or you aren't doesn't make you better or worse. It's just one of those things you MUST discover. If you are an empathic soul, and you are pretending you are not, you are easy prey for the shadow archetypes like the addict, the codependent empath, the perfectionist, and the victim. These archetypes come on board to help, often in youth to help us survive, but usually end up causing dysfunction of mind, body, and spirit. The key is to get radically honest with yourself and ask, "Do I hide who I am at my core? If yes, why?" If you were completely anonymous, what would you do? Say? Write? How would you love?

Think about your day. Are you on the hamster wheel? Why? Do you feel like you have a choice? Why or why not? During Covid Season, even as everything came to a halt, did you still find a way to be in motion? I know I did.

Light Lift 3: Zip Up

Stand up straight, feet shoulder width apart. As if you were zipping up a jacket, zip up from your pelvic region to your chin tracing your fingers along your body all the way to your chin along the middle of your body. The idea is to zip up through your energy centers, your chakras, but leave open the top and bottom as your connections to the planet. You want to protect yourself for sensory overload, while keeping yourself connected at the same time. I write this one on my daily Google calendar and if I forget to do it, you can see me in the middle of Target, standing still and zipping up!

CHAPTER FOUR:

Dusting the Buddha

The quieter you become, the more you hear.

—Ram Dass

I've always been struck by how our differences create beauty and how we have this strand of commonality that we all share. Both are true. Examples can be found in the threads that runs through all the world's religions. This realization came to me the first time I celebrated Passover. Having grown up in a strict Southern Baptist town where my Sunday school teacher warned my mom I would go to hell if I missed Sunday school, I only learned of one religion. All others were considered wrong and a one-way ticket to hell. But when my husband and I started dating, and he invited me to Aunt Ruthy's house for my first Passover Seder, I was struck by the common symbols between Passover, Good Friday, and Easter. How did I not know about this combination before? The Seder was 50-person strong and there was an emphasis on the children, with the youngest reader reading the questions. There was the hiding of the matzah that the children were supposed to find, just like hiding the eggs with a prize at the end (often money) for all my Easters. There was an egg on the Seder plate. Special foods were made, just as they were during Easter. An emphasis on escaping suffering colored each event. At Passover, the theme was to recognize how the Jewish people were enslaved and how not to do that in current life. At Easter, the emphasis was on how Jesus (a Jew), suffered and rose again so that humans could remember that and not have to suffer themselves. Suffering by proxy. Comparing these two events in my head that night led me on a lifelong search to find those threads across religions that connect us rather than focusing on the parts that cause wars and hate. This seemed important.

Perhaps paradoxically, I'm not religious. Much of the time I find religions cruel at worst and hypocritical at best. Simultaneously, there is such beauty in the stories, in the symbols, in the rituals, and I've chased a clearer understanding of that thread in true seeker fervor. One of those chasings led me to the Mt. Shasta Abbey, a beautiful monastery in the shadow of Mt. Shasta, California, where female and male monks have created a beautiful space that feels whole, kind, and peaceful.

At this monastery, one can go and learn about Buddhism and all the lingo that goes with that. Really, you learn about community, ritual, and a different way of doing things. The setting is breathtaking. After winding down a road of majestic evergreens that reach so high in sky with their deep green pine-needled arms that you can barely see the indigo blue shining through, you turn into a gate and park next to trees with trunks the size of Montana. Statues of Kwan Yin and Buddha greet you, as they do throughout the property. Kwan Yin, the Goddess of Compassion who pours mercy on the earth, is palpable here and the first time I ever spent time with her over days was in this space. She has stayed with me since, very much a partner in my work around youth mental health, guiding and directing me where to pivot. Depending on the season, the abbey grounds cast a varying hue, all of them transformative in their own ways. I experienced the hue of spring. The bright red poppies stick out in my memory, but flowers were everywhere in crisp purples, oranges, petite pink blossoms, and green filling all the gaps in between. It was at this abbey that I spent days at a silent retreat, which any person can apply to do despite their religion or lack thereof.

The reason I wanted to spend days in silence was to become a better listener. I noticed I had developed (or maybe always had) the habit of interrupting. It wasn't that I was trying to think of what I was going to say next as all the "be a better listener" books I read said, but rather I'd get so excited while listening to someone else speak, I wanted to join in. Or, maybe I was kidding myself. Either way, I knew it was annoying and I wanted to learn to listen better, to hear someone deeply, a trait I felt was missing in the world. I was craving that type of listening in my own life and I knew I must learn this new skill to give this important gift to both myself and others.

Going in, I knew relatively nothing other than I was going on a silent retreat. I didn't know we would be waking every day at 5:00 a.m. for our first meditation. I didn't know that in that morning, after meditation and silent group meals and prayer, I would have chores. I didn't know that after that there would be two more meditation sections, dharma talks about life, or any of it. I just entered with a beginner's mind.

When it came to my duties, I was given the task of knocking down spider webs, which I struggled with because of an injured shoulder and because it seemed out of line with the philosophy of not killing things. I wasn't a Buddhist, but I do believe in reincarnation, and always want to cover my bases just in case. I also just really don't like killing things. Growing up in the country, my stepbrother Aaron took me out to learn to shoot guns when I was about six. I remember barely being able to hold the rifle. Out in the middle of the field, we started with bottles for the aiming practice, then graduated to squirrels. When it was time to shoot the squirrel, I couldn't do it. I felt like I was going to vomit. I hated everything about it, but especially the way it made me feel. The monks at the retreat kindly gave me another job: dusting the Buddha.

They showed me into the temple where we went to do our multiple meditation sessions each day, sessions I came to adore. This temple was sacred space. It was full of that feeling when you walk into a spiritual space. That palpable emotional current when you step off the airplane onto the runway at the Kona Airport and feel the land reach up to kiss your feet. This was that. The monk showed me my task in front of me, to dust the whole – I don't know what it's called – gigantic space behind where ceremony was held in the front of the temple. A huge platform with the largest golden Buddha I've ever seen sat up there and I was to dust it and the whole area around it. The monk left, and I was in this glorious, quiet space all alone. Just me, Buddha, and millions of prayers before me.

I climbed up on the platform from a ladder in the back with my supplies. This was no longer a chore. A feeling of gratitude and connection came over me. I didn't have to be a Buddhist to feel it. It wasn't about tribal thinking or religious construct. This was so completely different than that. This was about borrowing that wonderful Buddhist notion of beginner's mind and entering into a space of calmly, thoroughly, intimately.

This was the most sacred of the spaces.

Light Lift 4: Finding Still

The word meditation has become a generic word that refers to many different ways of becoming still. The first part of the word "med" means to "take appropriate measures." The goal here is to not proclaim one type of meditation superior over another, but rather to "take appropriate measures" to finding stillness. We live in a microwave world that wants what it wants now, and our wiring often matches that. If you are new to the world of meditation, take it slowly and be patient with yourself. Here is how to start.

Sit anywhere (your car, the park, the bathroom) you can find space. Set your phone timer for 2 minutes and put it out of your reach. You can do anything for 2 minutes, right? Then sit and repeat "inhale" and "exhale" as you breathe deeply in and out. Do this each morning, adding an additional minute when you're ready.

Your goal, here, is to develop a habit of finding stillness once a day, every day, to start. Give it as much importance as your sleep, your exercise, your free time. If you're always looking for an extra edge like me, build up to two times daily for 20 minutes per session. This will change your life in ways you cannot even imagine.

CHAPTER FIVE:

Synchroni-City

We must remember that the rationalistic attitude of the West is not the only possible one and is not all-embracing but is in many ways a prejudice and a bias that ought perhaps to be corrected.

—C.G. Jung

At the sacred Mt. Shasta Abbey, finding "still" can be almost a cliché. For me, that cliché worked. However, at this point in my life, I have a much more difficult time finding this in cities. Frequently, those who love the city can't imagine a more sacred space than capturing an early morning dawn over a New York City skyline. The first time I saw that skyline, I saw it from the inside. I was 18 and walked through the city with my head thrown all the way back in search of the tops of those buildings which reached as high as the evergreens in the redwood forests of Mt. Shasta. The connectivity of the buildings, and how on one city block, there are more businesses and people than there were in my whole town growing up, is its own kind of sacred space. I get, and appreciate, this idea of urban space.

While at UCLA, I fell in love with the City of Angels during an urban architecture class. It was a small class, which I loved, because not all of them were. We had many field trips to old buildings, and historic neighborhoods in many different pockets of LA. I learned how urban architects attempt to create sacred space with green space and various zoning laws. My final project was studying the language of gang culture and how they used street art to claim their space. This got me into some sticky situations when I was taking pictures of those spaces, as I recall.

What the city offers for sure are so many opportunities to learn about synchronicity. Because so much is happening energetically and in the physical world simultaneously in that space, a glance around connects past to present, local to international, differences to similarities, wealth to poverty, all firing hand-in-hand. I'm in love with that part of cities. I remember one time being in Sedona on vacation and a woman told me I should look out for a class on this esoteric topic I had never heard of before. When I arrived home, I found out the class was being offered within walking distance from our home, directly next door to my favorite sushi place and nail salon. I followed that synchronicity; it changed my life.

Why do we want to learn about synchronicity? Because by learning to awaken, to consciously spot the connections our Universe offers us, we understand on a very personal level how everything is interconnected. Here's an example that came up just as I was rewriting this chapter.

I had a dream that was a bit unusual for me. It was a "chasing" dream. My friend Sadie and I were being chased by a man with a frog growing out of his foot. We were running hard to get away and Sadie was faster, so I hopped on her back and she carried me. Then I remembered: in chasing dreams, you need to stop, turn, and ask, "Why are you trying to get my attention right now?" We then sat down and had a very nice conversation with the frog-leg man and got to know him and his frog.

I woke up and told my husband I had an unusual dream outside my normal landscape about a man with a frog growing out of his foot. Here's the synchronicity. As I was deadheading the rose bush outside my window less than an hour later, I found a tiny frog nestled in a leaf sleeping so soundly five feet from where I dreamed about the frog man. I am a disciple of Synchronicity because of how I see it can help people, so I then posted it on Facebook and tagged my friend Sadie.

Turns out, she'd been swimming recently, mostly with a frog kick. In fact, the day before she sent a picture to another friend of a frog, with a picture of it kicking. Another friend told me *frog* could be my animal totem, which reminded me of my additional dream the night before about a large talking frog leading me down a path. I looked up *frog* and this is what it said:

The frog represents feminine energy, ease in transition, emotional and spiritual cleansing, and exploring life in all its wonder. No matter what stage of life you feel you're in, you can count on the frog spirit animal to guide you in many different areas of your life.

As it turns out, I was heading out on a 21-Day Blog Tour across the West Coast which was indeed filled with wonder and guidance. Add to this the following comments from my friends playing the synchronicity game who were navigated to different truths, both for me and themselves. Some took place in public, and even more took place in private. They fired throughout the day. Frog not only showed up for me, but simply by me sharing this with others, it showed up for them, too.

Life becomes so much fun and so much more meaningful when we romp on the playground of synchronicity. About ten years ago, when understanding this concept really struck me as the key to individual happiness, I went around asking all my friends if they would be my synchronicity friends. When the inevitable next question about what the hell that meant came up, I would explain that the more we see these signs and share them, the more fun and meaning we find in life. I would get a number of reactions: (1) *The Glaze*, a look I get from my friends when they think I've clearly gone off into Pisces Land where they don't really want to go or (2) "I don't want to disappoint you if I don't have enough synchronicities." As a result, I never landed on a very good match that stuck for long, nor did I find anyone who cared to stick around and understand the value this practice has to offer. I continue my search.

To this day, I have only become more certain that this is a key to understanding your personal space – your sacred space – in the world. When you find this space, this doesn't mean all is smooth wind-in-the-hair, face-in-the-sun sailing. If life was all the same weather all the time, how boring would that be? What it does mean, though, is that you get this strengthening of intuitive guidance system (IGS) that works with the signs in the world to navigate you to your True North.

Light Lift 5: Become a Synchronicity Detective

If you're new to synchronicity spotting, here's your first case. Use a beginner's mind and open up to the idea that this synchronicity thing will be a treasure map to much fun and joyful navigation in your life. Pay close attention to things that you might think of as coincidence. Are you thinking about your friend you haven't talked to for a month right when she calls? Start there. Write them down, either in the notes on your phone or in a journal.

If you're a veteran at synchronicities, amp it up and follow the thread. The more you notice, the more you'll receive. They're like dreams that way. At some point, you just laugh out loud by the magic of it all. Collecting synchronicities is not only joyful, it can connect you to the reason you're here on the planet in live time. Collectively, synchronicity maps make you shine so bright, when others try to dim your light, they won't be able to anymore.

CHAPTER SIX:

You-Nique

No one is you and that is your power.

—Dave Grohl

O ne of the key concepts we can teach our children is that their role in this world, their unique fingerprint, is different from anyone else's. We each have a unique gift to bring to the world that breathes outside tribal thinking, family of origin, and all the constructs we try to throw over our newborns as we dress them in binary clothes and give them toys we want them to play with because that was done to us. It's what the tribe expects. Imagine what each child, given the permission to really shine who they are at their core, would be if allowed to do this for themselves. Because we are students of the lessons taught, this can be hard to accomplish, but imagine what the world would be like if we moved forward in that direction.

If you could be anything, if anything was possible, what would you be? Sometimes we ask this question to children who often parrot back what they feel is the acceptable response. I remember this question from my own youth. I often told everyone I wanted to be a lawyer because that seemed to make people react positively in some way. Had I admitted I wanted to be a writer, or that I could actually have a main job as a writer, I'm not sure I would have gotten the same encouragement.

For this reason, I am a huge advocate of mentoring. When I was in middle school, I had a counselor who believed in me and gave me a vision I did not have for myself. As an adult, I have made an effort to pay that forward with my children, with my students, and with young people I have mentored along the way. One of those people is Ellie.

Ellie came to a book signing for my book *First Break*. Her Grandma Ellen brought her. About a month later, she sent me an email and told me she wanted to get into UCLA as a transfer student and asked if I could take a look at her admission's essay. This began the process of me learning about Ellie's uniqueness, her amazing spark as an artist. She was a storyteller, first wanting to tell stories with tattoos on skin, and then wanting to tell stories with paint on walls. She wanted to tell stories that were hard to tell, and she had an ability to do it. Over the past four years of watching Ellie emerge into what I see will be a world-famous muralist and university graduate, the first in her family, I am convinced she will make the world a brighter place with her art. She has already started mentoring others and continues to recruit mentors to help herself. It's a beautiful cycle.

One of the books I give to almost every person younger than 25, and found it myself about that age when I was working at a high-paying job in law firms where I was miserable, is *What Color is Your Parachute?* This bible to understanding your strengths, talents, weaknesses, what matters to you, and basically what you should be doing with your life, has been updated so many times I don't even know what version it's on and it doesn't matter. When I read that book, it gave me what I think is missing in trying to figure out who you are and your life purpose. It gave me hope and vision about my place in the world.

We are not taught this in school, or at least I wasn't. Our education system always seems to have its own identity crisis, which I really noticed during my Master of Arts in Teaching work. Nobody seemed to be able to agree on the simplest things like how to teach children to read or how to teach them math. The theories were always changing. Camps of people lined up behind walls of whole language, phonics, new math, old math, whatever textbook companies were pushing. Discovering who uniquely you are? Well, the curriculum didn't allow time for that.

Instead, that would have to be found in all the extra-curricular junk we throw our kids in with the hope that something will stick (or, worst case, they will have a strong college application with four years of something that looked like they liked it) and they can find who they really are that way. Then, one thing leads to another, and pretty soon they find themselves waking up to a whole new reality as Shadyac and Carrey did.

Circling back, Shadyac had an awakening when he traveled the world making "I Am." It helped that he was able to have the world classroom, that he had the money to go and talk to all the world's luminaries and in that time and sacred space, really learn that as a species, we are naturally about collaboration, not competition, as he'd been taught. He's got a new gig now, surrounded by young mentees, back in the film space in a new state, but with a different flare based on his conscious awakening about what's important and who he is, a new sacred space emerging.

Who are you? What is your calling? These are such hard questions; one friend shudders when I ask and changes the subject immediately. Distraction is much more comfortable for her in the short run, but I keep asking because I feel deeper happiness and joy lies on the other side of that awkward wall, and we want to get there. This isn't just for your own happiness and joy, but that of the world, because as we've seen, we're all connected. When you take a moment to really ask yourself those questions and get to the answer, you not only help yourself, you help all of us – and all of us we really need you deeply.

Light Lift 6: Know Thy You-nique Self

This is a starting point. Take this free character survey to determine your key strengths. It will take about 20 minutes. There is an extended survey you can pay for, but the free test is quite sufficient to start. Next, buy *What Color is Your Parachute?* and do the exercises there. I've bought that book for nearly every mentee I've ever had, including my own children. This link will get you to the survey: https://www.viacharacter. org/reports

CHAPTER SEVEN:

In Your Own Backyard

If I ever go looking for my heart's desire...

—*The Wonderful Wizard of Oz,* MGM 1939

In MGM's adaptation of Frank L. Baum's *Oz* books, Dorothy of Oz started off upset, restless, angry at the lady who wanted to get rid of her dog. She then ended up in a fantasy land, a "waking-up" while she slept, spending her whole journey trying to get to the person who could help her get back home. A bit obsessed really (not so much in Baum's version as in MGM's version), we heard her say *There's no place like home* ad nauseum. When we finally come to the end, we learn that everything she needed was in her own backyard.

And, here we are. We are sheltering in place, an invitation from The Covid. Whether out of fear or out of curiosity about this growing idea, a seed shortage shows that many have gone back to basics and are growing things. There is not only a rush of this seed-purchasing in rural areas, but also growing sprouts in city apartments and small spaces. My oldest son and his partner, college professors teaching from home, have rediscovered childhood skills like painting and making so many different kinds of foods with bananas and toasted coconut I can't even keep up. My youngest son, a college senior, is finishing up his term in a Zoom classroom, learning how to exercise in a new way, and how to live in close quarters with roommates when going out isn't much of an option. He's learning to be still when he wants to get going. We're all searching for our own way to make our own backyards, metaphorical and literal, work for us.

I hear some say, "I just go from Zoom to Zoom. I'm busier now than I was before." Being both underproductive and over productive are coping skills. Looking at which slot you fall into is good information, not to be judged, but to be met with compassion and further knowing about yourself. Do you get rabidly busy (guilty!) or do you have a hard time getting going? Know that about yourself and let it be in the room.

This opportunity to step outside into spring and listen is such a precious invitation. The space between the chimes tinkling in the wind. The space between the white puffy clouds shifting from a dinosaur to a dolphin jumping in the sky against an indigo canvas. The deep purple Iris blooming into new life. The fragrance of the roses opening to share their spring aroma. The waters around the world so clean the dolphins are jumping in multi-pods off the California coast and swimming through the Venice canals of Italy. People report the Ganges River is clean enough to drink. The sky shines brighter than any of us have ever seen. The Sea Turtles, the Honu, thrive in the Hawaiian waters where the reefs are rebuilding themselves at algorithmic rates. In such a short period of time we have come into this glorious new earth.

Yet, we aren't just learning romantic lessons from the garden. When Wuhan re-opened, they say the divorce lines down the street were long. I thought about this a lot. Relationships are hard, and often are about facing our darkest corners. They say what irritates you about your spouse is a reflection of your own something, whether it's a lack of your own self-worth, a belief or fear that keeps you in a relationship long past the expiration date, or just junk that's not been worked out and may never be. Depending where you are in the course of a relationship, the beginning, middle, and end all have their strengths and weaknesses. I think what those long lines showed was that when we were forced in close spaces where distraction could no longer prolong a relationship, many realized this was the change they needed to make.

Change, though. It can be a sparring partner, sometimes for reasons we don't even know. We get used to things. We get comfortable. Maybe it's not fantastic, we say. We justify, but it's familiar. I know what to expect. That predictability is comfortable. Next comes the fear of the unknown: if I made the change, would it be great, or would it be awful? Would it be a mistake, or would it be the best thing to happen in my life? All those mental gymnastics are enough to create a mental lockdown and land us in the ever-fated land of analysis paralysis.

During the 2020 Lockdown, which morphed and shifted into many versions of power and powerlessness, I noticed a huge uptick in mental health issues. Statistically, we saw a rise and saw media personalities come out, saying they were suffering from various forms of mental illness. I also saw this happening in my closest circles, and as the isolation extended, symptoms increased. As a nation, my country saw a spike in racial injustice and tensions arising out of that space. An unprecedented election year pitted neighbor against neighbor and "fear" seem to be a concept everyone was feeling in one form or another. In some moments, this feeling of being trapped in a crucible of tension felt unbearable. Add to that, my whole state of California was burning, and each day felt a bit like a bad apocalyptic "B" movie.

And yet, here we are back to the gifts of The Covid. The Covid, if asked, would say, "Hey. It's not me. It's you." The Covid would be right. It's not the thing itself, whatever that thing is, it's the reaction to the thing itself that wants the control. FEAR.

False Evidence Appearing Real, or a mechanism that keeps us protected from the tigers in our proverbial jungles. It can be a bugger that steals people's joy and keeps them from taking time to see the magic of the moment. At times in my life, I feel fearless, but with all transparency I can say this period of time was not one of them.

Right now, whichever space you are in, *you* are the sacred space. It's okay not to be okay. You just need to stay. In the same way the smoke eventually cleared, whatever season you are in will pass, too. Beautiful destruction, my younger son called it. Desolation and resilience as new growth bursts forward. It all gets to be in the room, and we are all connected to both.

After you read this sentence, close your eyes and listen to all the noises you can hear. Breathe in this precious air and all the smells it gifts us. Taste the possibility of the garden. The green strawberries shifting to red. Feel the air against your skin. Take all this in, exactly as it is and exactly as you are. Write these sensations down in the notepad of your mind. Whether the sounds of all the different kinds of birds singing with the chimes blowing in the wind as a dog barks in the distance, or a city horn honking as a siren screeches by, listen. Listen as if you are on a silent retreat. Listen deeply as you would to a friend you so desperately love. Study all this with your mind as if you are dusting the Buddha meticulously. Sit with the moment, this perfect moment, no matter what. Here, you have made sacred space. Here, you shine.

Light Lift 7 - Listen Deeply to the Voice Behind the Voice

For one minute, close your eyes and listen. Name everything you hear, including your own deep intuition. Let it in. Savor it. All of it.

CHAPTER EIGHT:

The Dolphins at Two-Step

Play.
Be curious.
Dive deep.
Rest.
Hang with the pod.
Bring the magic.
Find your life's porpoise.
Jump!
Love, Dolphin

When the world opens up again, the place I most want to be is on the Big Island of Hawaii. We consider this a second home and spend weeks there several times a year. From the moment my feet touch the tarmac, I feel Gaia herself reaching up to hold me. The scent of plumeria hits me even as the hot asphalt competes, but never wins. The flowers are too strong. The island breezes, gentle to raging, predict the mood of Pele herself. As we begin the drive down the stunning coastline, wind chases my hair because you cannot really appreciate the island fully any other way. Turquoise waters wave, welcoming us back home.

Places that call on the island, sacred spaces, come with dolphins. I am saddened though by those who exploit the dolphins, whales, rays, many of them with non-eco-friendly tours because I empathize with the dolphins in the wild and don't like the idea of their rest being disturbed by the desire of companies to make money off chasing them. I am saddened by those who chase them. I won't do that. This has been an evolving thing for me over the years, much like a person chooses to become a vegetarian because they simply don't feel right about eating meat anymore.

Still, I adore dolphins, really am pretty sure I should have been a mermaid in this lifetime instead of a human and am more at home in the sea than anywhere else in the world. The sea is my sacred space and the dolphins and whales light up every cell in my body when I feel them nearby. I love to be near them, to share energy. It sparkles and brings me giggly joy unlike any other.

On the last day of one trip, we were eating breakfast at a local joint we love and a server we had become fond of asked us what we were doing that day. We hadn't really decided, wanted to let synchronicity lead the way. It came in her words.

"I've heard the dolphins are down at Two-Step."

Two-Step is a snorkeling spot called such because of the two rock steps etched into the tide pools which allows for a fairly simple entry into the ocean kingdom. It is not easy beach entry as down in Hapuna Beach State Park or the popular white sand beaches. In fact, there is very little sand and swimmers sun themselves on lava rock as locals sit nearby and protectively oversee the area. The dolphins rest in the bay just out from the cove. We could catch them before their nap. The journey there was a long one, about an hour-and-a-half from where we stayed, but also offered an opportunity to us to say good-bye to the Island for a few months. We hopped in the car and took the long drive to Two-Step and arrived ready to snorkel.

When we reached the tide pool, we could see pods of dolphins playing out in the distance. Giddy joy shot through me at the sight. It was one of those great days when hardly anybody was around except a few younger kids paddling around in the water. A nearby resident was playing the soundtrack "Ocean Dreams" which I recognized as I had frequently played that for my second graders at Pacific Elementary in Manhattan Beach, California when they were writing. It helped them create. I thought about the lessons I'd taught on whales and sea life, the ecosystems, the joy and curiosity that young learners approach such things. I loved teaching about them, but even more, I loved the idea of swimming in the wild with them.

As we slid into the warm, tropical water and began to glide through the bay, tropical fish of purples, yellows, blues, and oranges played tag beneath us. The world beneath the water mesmerizes me, and in this moment, I could feel a tingling rush through my body from my toes to my head. The closer we moved to the dolphins, the more intense it got. And then, a mix of emotions: curiosity, caution, reckless abandon, a desire to live in this ocean and never return to land. Closer still, I became aware that there were not just a few dolphins, but multiple pods of wild dolphins. While initially I was fearless, it occurred to me maybe I shouldn't be. These were wild animals, after all. I had just started developing an obsession for underwater filming at the time so had my Go-Pro with me and let my desire to film overtake my cautious pause.

As my camera started, we sensed it was time to pause. Rather than swimming to the dolphins, we stopped and treaded water in place. We looked up at the young swimmers chasing the majestic mammals and watched the dolphins swim away. They were coming straight for us at a rapid rate. Before we knew it, pods of dolphins surrounded us and a feeling of complete joy engulfed me. There was no longer fear, but an uncontainable joy. I turned around and around in a circle giggling, dipping underneath the water to catch a glimpse of a young baby clearly wanting to put on a show with the leaf game. It would dive down deep and come up to put a leaf on its nose as its mom spotted off to the right. It was one of the most amazing moments of my life. All I could do was giggle. You can actually see this footage if you go to my YouTube Channel and I will never, ever take it down.

It was as if the dolphins rewarded us for living our last day synchronistically. From the café to Two-Step to waiting for them to come to us because that's what our intuitive hears said to do, they filled our hearts with joy and I wondered how to bottle that and bring it back. That moment taught me the value of deeply listening to my heart, and the magic that lies ahead when I do.

Light Lift 8 - Daily Dolphin Energy

Add some energy exercises into your daily routine. Here's the first one.

Stand, preferably outside barefoot on the grass, but work with what you have. Take your three middle fingers on each hand and tap underneath your cheeks. Do this for about 15 seconds. Next, find the place where both collarbones meet and tap with your three middle fingers there for 15 seconds. Finally, find the area just above your sternum and pound your chest like Tarzan for 15 seconds. This is a routine I have added to my morning ritual and find it just brings that jolt of dolphin energy I want to carry with me always.

CHAPTER NINE:

Trust Holes -
Find 'em and Fill 'em

*"The best way to find out if you can trust
somebody is to trust them."*

—Ernest Hemingway

Words are so much easier than the actions needed to cement those words in place. Saying *let the dolphins come to you* instead of chasing them may imply a completely passive role. This is not the intention. We must actively participate in a receptive way. To do this, we must trust in a Universe that has our back. But if it hasn't before, if it has betrayed us, how can we trust it again?

The best way to do this is to work on our stuff. In my experience, those who don't think they have any stuff usually have the most to work on. We all have stuff that needs to be cleared, and admitting that is the first step. If we can't admit it, that's another issue, and creates a huge block to further movement and happiness for the soul. This results in suppression, which will pop out in other ways, usually along with cousins Guilt and Shame, as the job to suppress (or compartmentalize) becomes far more work than it would have been just to unravel the junk in the first place. Sort of like hoarding so much stuff that the idea of cleaning it out becomes overwhelming. Additionally, the reward at the end is your own happiness and peace, which means more happiness and peace for everyone you are connected with – which means all of us.

I learned this in depth when I went through practitioner training to become a licensed practitioner in the Centers for Spiritual Living. I ended up there in a synchronistic drive-by that happened one day when we moved back to Northern California from Southern California in 2008.

It was an errand day, and I was taking a shortcut to Costco. Suddenly, I heard one of those nudgings, this intuitive feeling that said so emphatically I couldn't suppress it, "Pull into this parking lot." I pulled in, rounded some shrubs blocking the entrance, and drove up to this building that definitely looked like what my friend Katie and ex-teaching partner would call a "Jamie Place." There were bright flowers, and statues of angels. There were water features and birds playing in the trees. Buddha was lifting his hands to the sky and laughing. Peace flags hung from two tall oaks that bordered a labyrinth. Roses in all colors framed a DG path to meander through, with water features bringing the flow of life to the scene. I parked my car and walked up to the building hearing clearly, "You will teach here. You are meant to teach here."

I still had no idea where "here" was or what happened here, but I was growing into this life by synchronicity practice and I knew that every time I listened, I won. I won a happiness hit for me and those around me. I won this feeling of peace I had searched for all my life. I won this absolute positive knowing that I was in flow and on the river floating in sync with the Universe.

Still, my stomach fluttered with a thousand butterfly wings. I reached for the door. I paused. I could turn back. I should – *no, don't should on yourself* – turn back. This whole presidential debate with me playing both candidates took place in that moment. Exasperated by the internal dialogue, I pulled the door and walked in. I spotted the office, put on my cheeriest smile, and said, "Hi, I'm Jamie. I just wanted to find out what you do here."

This lady stood up and looked down on me. She seemed seven feet tall in her long flowing deep purple robe-like clothes. My face went hot. This flowy patchwork purple velvet was majestic, but it also reminded me of something the cult leader in San Diego who had everyone go catch the spaceship after he poisoned them might wear. My shoulders tightened, but still I was intrigued, and wanted to understand why synchronicity led me here. I knew it was my job to stay curious and figure out this puzzle. As I talked with the lady in the long velvet purple robe dress, I blurted out something like, "I think I'm supposed to teach here." And then, there it was: *The Glaze.* She stood up.

"Well, it was great meeting you."

I stood up and stumbled over my chair in a rush to escape, knowing I said the wrong thing. I hopped in my car, cursing my voice behind the voice that brought me here, asking it how I could trust it if it was going to lead me into awkwardly strange experiences like that without any clear directions. I decided this synchronicity and intuition business was messed up. I did not go back to The Center for a year.

What I've learned about this guidance, though, is that it is relentless and will keep visiting in different venues until I listen. Sure enough, I was at a TedX event in Redding, California watching speakers speak, minding my own business, when my friend Katie (a different Katie) ran up to me and said, "Oh my gosh. I've been thinking about you. I'm teaching a writing class and you have to come."

"Of course. When?" I asked.

"It started last week but come tomorrow. You're not too late to catch up," she said and went to hurry off, yelling back, "It's at the Center for Spiritual Living in Redding."

Oh no. The robe place. Too late. I'd already agreed. I would go straight to the writing class, not stop at the purple robe lady, who I soon found out wasn't there anymore. After the writing class, I signed up for a next class and a next class. Then, I taught a class on where "Film and Spirituality Intersect" and how we can create a better world using film. I became a licensed practitioner, going through four years of classes and intense practitioner training. I taught another class on depression and anxiety with my mentor, Reverend Sue. I spent a glorious period of years learning who I was and how to listen deeply to others (though my kids would argue I need even more classes.) Through following this synchronicity (finally, again), I learned about the deep holes in my trust, why they might be there, and more importantly, how to stop them up, so they didn't hemorrhage out all my joy.

One of those holes came in the form of trust in women. I had no idea why, and all I wanted to do was experience the nurturing comfort and mentorship from women that I saw so many others come to so easily. I could feel, back in 2010, a need for the Feminine Rising (in all genders) and I knew I must deal with this trust issue by getting to the bottom of it. For as long as I could remember, I was afraid of women, especially in groups. I steered very clear of sororities in college for this reason. When I was very young, I remember diving under chairs to hide when moms would come pick up their kids at the babysitter. Even then, I was aware of a difference of my own safe space around women and how it didn't exist there and yet I craved it. As I moved into the business world, my boss wanted me to join professional women's organizations, as he felt this would be good for my own development and for the law firm where I did marketing and client relations. I would physically get ill each time I had to go into those meetings and could never figure out why.

I knew I had trust issues that had piled up over the years, betrayals from friends, back stabs throughout all my years. I didn't seem alone there, but other women seemed to move past that. I knew this was a trust hole I needed to fill, but I just didn't know how to do it. I felt weird talking about it, lest I play into a self-fulfilling prophecy and never find the type of female bonding I saw everyone else make happen so easily. When I walked into my first session of practitioner training with the group that would be my cohort for the next two years on a weekly basis, you guessed it, all women. In the opening circle, I felt that nudge to say my truth. I felt I needed to be brave and admit this thing I had, even if my face got hot and my stomach felt like it could betray me at any moment. I blurted it out and hoped I wouldn't get *The Glaze: I have to tell you all, I have trust issues when it comes to women.*

When I put myself in their shoes, I laugh. They must have been thrilled. Over that next two years I would find myself being held by that group of women like I never have before. I grew to love each of them deeply as they helped me through that journey, accepting me just as I was, a rebel who doesn't do religion of any kind well and wants to talk about both shadow and light. It was not a linear journey by any means, and I would find myself in multiple new groups of women for various reasons over that two-year period. I would still feel betrayed. I would still feel hurt. But I learned to question it, and talk it through when it made sense, minimally to spot issues early and set boundaries. I discovered by going deeply into this willingness to look at my own holes in my trust, a crucial space that needed addressing, Spirit would lead me to answers I so craved.

This journey, and exercises done in the training, opened up a conversation with my mom where I shared my heart and told her I just didn't understand where these issues came from. She shared a story with me that I think she probably struggled to share. As a mom you want to remember your moves in all the right light as you love your babies so much and want to make sure you do everything you can to help them grow to happy, healthy humans who can make the world a better place for being in it. Part of that is being vulnerable with your own children, and on that day she was.

She told me that one of my early babysitters was a woman with multiple children who decided to babysit me for extra money but was really more concerned about her own children. She had an assistant, a young woman, who witnessed the neglect of this woman toward me. It bothered the young woman so much that she quit her job and contacted my mom. As soon as my mom found out, she pulled me out of the daycare, but apparently some early imprinting had already happened. I think about that and wonder why it wasn't the woman who saved me that I remember, and I think that is because I never knew that part. I only knew at some subconscious level about the woman who neglected and hurt me.

Recently, I found myself on a heart-opening call when my dear friend Haumea was being interviewed about her work. At the time she was in Bali for a month. I wanted to support her in her interview. The woman who interviewed her had other guests, all women, who were talking about this whole trust issue with other women. It was the same dynamic I had felt all my life. They were so open and honest, and what I realized is that while everyone wasn't blurting it out, many women had these exact same issues. It's just that we were taught to be nice, not to talk about it, to get along, to be good girls. Because of this molding by society and how gender plays into those constructs, so clearly illustrated in *The Handmaid's Tale* by Margaret Atwood and visually illustrated in the series, women have historically been forced into a competition against each other for their very survival. This competition weighs us all down, making each feel like they are alone. At one job, I had a female boss who was bullying me like I had never been bullied and when I reached out to my peer whom I thought was a friend, she said, "I'm sorry. I can't side with you here. This same thing happened to me at my old job and when I did what was right and stood up, I got bullied even worse and lost my job. I can't afford to lose this job. We can't talk anymore."

Recently, while in the Village of Oak Creek near Sedona, Arizona, I saw a young woman wearing a hat. She was with two other women and they seemed to have a bond I've always sought to have with women. I asked her if I could take a picture of her black ski cap. She smiled and said of course. Embroidered in white were these words: *Empowered Women Empower Women.*

Thank you, Universe. The trust holes are filling up.

Light Lift 9 - Empower Hour

Spend an hour with yourself getting honest about your own patterns. Pick one theme that has followed you throughout your life. What is your earliest memory about the theme? Write about it. When you're ready, share it with someone who listens well to see if any more clarity comes in. Then, have a dialogue with it in writing. Ask it how it has served you. Ask it how it has disempowered you. Interview it with objective curiosity. You may find an opening that will leave you feeling more empowered than you ever could have been before.

CHAPTER TEN:

Face it: You're Worth It

"You, yourself, as much as anybody in the entire universe, deserve your love and affection."

—Buddha

We are conditioned, depending on our age and upbringing, to think taking care of ourselves first is selfish when actually it is the best thing we can do, both for ourselves and for the world. We hear this all the time, but to put it into practice becomes quite difficult for so many of us.

What does this look like though, this radical self-care that seems to be popping up in so many of my emails during the Covid time? We're back to finding sacred spaces, but this time not on another land, or in a favorite escape, but instead within us. When I look at Aubrey, I can see she is an incredible writer with a promising future and that she will likely write the work that changes the world. Aubrey, though, can't see that in herself because she's gone into survival mode as she weaves her way through the dark night of her Soul. Anthony was not able to make it out of that dark night, as he'd also lost that spark he had when he was near the ocean. The most interesting thing about Anthony that I learned when I went to his Life Celebration was that he saw the unique beauty in everyone else, but not in himself. I learned that from one his classmates, who asked if she could sit by me and when we exchanged stories, she told me Anthony's first words to her in high school were, "You are so beautiful. Can I draw you?"

What is this thing within us that blinds us to the You-nique beings each of us is? What is it that outlines the narrative of our low self-worth or lack of self-confidence or lack of ability to understand our life purpose when it's so clear to others? This is part of the waking-up thing. Becoming conscious is not just waking up to see in others, to understand the world, to read *A Course in Miracles*, start meditation, get involved in yoga, and travel to sacred places where we can get a hit off the land. Becoming conscious begins with you in your own backyard. It begins with you waking up to the beauty of who you really are, not what others have decided for you, though weeding through that is certainly part of the process.

Still, there is fear. Even in writing this book, it sits on my shoulder as my spirituality, while the core of who I am, has never been the thing I have shared openly in a book format. In my head spins the thought that I am a young-adult writer of fiction, not a non-fiction self-help, mind-body-spirit writer. When I open this dialogue with myself, I realize how ridiculous that is. I blogged for a decade, have 300 pages of metaphysical musings I shared with the world. Yet, there's a fear in me that writing it in a book is just not something I do. It doesn't make sense, these fears we feel. Others won't necessarily get them because they are so personal, and we won't get them either, unless we bravely take a moment to look at our own stuff. But here's what I've learned about those fears from a book I read a long time ago, popular when I was in high school, called *Feel the Fear and Do it Anyway* by Susan Jeffers. In fact, use the fear as a sign from your Internal Guidance System ("IGS") that this is the thing you most need to do. Then run to it, yelling, "I am fierce! I am brave! I am invincible!"

How to do this is so often sold in cookie-cutter programs with numbers: 7 ways to do this, 10 steps to get there, 5 levels to lift here. These programs exist because they are easy to market, and they are easy to package for marketing. However, just as you are unique so will the way you get there be unique. For many this process begins when they are hit upside the head with the 2x4. The best plan is to cave early before the 2x4 comes, because it will if you don't. In order to cave early, you have to listen. In order to listen, we need to hear. In order to hear, we need to be quiet. And now we're back to dusting the Buddha.

If you choose to ignore your own self-care, here's what you need to know. The Universe has your back and will be "encouraging" you to get where you need to go on your own journey. As individuals, and as a world, we get shoves from the Universe to move in certain ways. Well, first we get whispers, then we get synchronicities, then we get shoves, then we get a two-by-four moment. In slow motion, it goes like this. When it's time for a change, we get our first hit. Perhaps it's a whisper in the ear or a tap on the shoulder. We become conscious of it, but maybe it feels too hard to leave the familiar not-so-great because it's comfortable. We have excuses. If we don't listen, the next step is more cinematic. Multiple signs appear and volley for attention. If we still ignore it, the next phase is more dramatic – and painful. If we still resist, the intensity grows, and before we know it, the dark night of the Soul is upon us.

The best idea, and least painful in the end, is to get in during the early whispering stages. *Cave early*, Lissa Rankin once told me at an Esalen retreat, a policy she lived by. As a global family, we are now in this space, with potential in the ether for a number of outcomes. As I write this, we are still reacting to The Covid, and whether or not we will listen to the messages it sends remains to be seen. However, as individuals, we can begin now moving to a place of peace, joy, and harmony in our lives to shine like never before.

Light Lift 10 - 1,2,3 Me

Self-care is as unique as you are, and what it looks like for you will not be what it looks like for me. You must define what it is for you. Write out 3 things that really charge you up. It can be as simple as sitting under a tree for 15 minutes uninterrupted, or as fancy as going to a destination spa. Make #1 something you can do any time you feel taxed out that's immediately available. Make #2 something special that excites you to plan. Make #3 something bigger you strive to do. Commit to putting your self-care in place immediately. Do something each day. Build your list. You deserve it, and the world needs you to do it.

CHAPTER ELEVEN:

Dream

We were together. I forget the rest.

—Walt Whitman

Paradoxically, one of the best ways to wake to new levels of consciousness is to dream while you sleep. In the dream world there are colors and a loosening of laws we don't have during the daytime. The unique colors I see at night leave me buzzing for days. Dreaming teaches me possibilities that are endless. I can breathe underwater. I can swim through caves into other worlds. I can fly high in the sky and have conversations with people I can't have in the waking hours. All of this doesn't just happen. I work at it. I study it. I take workshops. I pay attention to dreaming as I would someone I love, and exercise my dream muscles just as I would if I were going to run a marathon.

I have this dream app that helps me increase my lucid dreaming by asking me about five times a day "Are you dreaming?" I hold up my hand, repeat the words, and see if my hand holds shape. In a dream, if you hold up your hand, it cannot hold shape, or it has a different number of fingers than usual. By training your subconscious mind to ask this question on a regular basis, you will be able to remember to ask yourself this at night in your dream. Once you do that, and realize you are dreaming, you can then do whatever you want in the dream. Fly. Breathe underwater. Help someone on the other side of the world. The more you honor that sacred space and use it wisely, the more opportunities you get to use it. (Leave the sex dreams for amateurs.)

Even though your path to your internal peace and healing is tailored to you, there are definite places you can pull for inspiration. Dreams are one of these. There are reams of books that talk about dreams: how to have them, what they mean, how we use them, how a world that has problems sleeping is supposed to dream, how we remember them, lucid dreams, and on and on. Even though I have studied dreams for 15 years, have had pre-cognitive dreams my entire life, have attended Stephen Eizenstat's *Dreamtending* workshops at Pacifica University near Santa Barbara, California, have run dream groups, have held dream seminars, and have participated in a worldwide dream-gathering event, I still have times when I go on dream breaks and give it a rest. However, dreams are one of the greatest resources we have to guide our daily lives and we can learn so much about ourselves through this process if we just stick with it.

An example of that was this book, which came to me in a dream with a clear title: *Chasing Sacred Spaces*. I had recently proclaimed I was not going to publish another book for a number of reasons and that title flashed over and over in my mind like a tortuous neon flashing light saying, "Oh yes you are, and here's the title." I woke up knowing I would make the choice to cave early and just do it. I had no idea what it was going to say, and honestly, I didn't think I had it in me. But as I've told you, it came pouring out over the course of that weekend in ways I couldn't have construed in my daylight hours and as it morphed and changed, I realized that its true calling was for each of us, you and me, to shine. I was to break all the rules of writing I had learned (*don't address the reader as you, don't share your own stories, don't make it too short/long/medium, don't self-publish*) and I was to allow my dreams to guide the metamorphosis of the work in the subsequent drafts. It became *Shine* after the conversation with a frog and my friend Sadie I mentioned earlier, when the frog (a symbol for metamorphosis) kept showing up to weigh in. Cave early.

This connection between night and day is something that fascinates me, and something I feel we are missing in our Western culture. It's a pathway to happiness. When I fly in a dream, I wake up empowered for the next two days. Yet, in talking to others about it, I realize dreaming is something many struggle with either because they don't care, they don't sleep well, certain medications affect their dream patterns, or they can't remember anything that happened. This makes connecting dreams to daily guidance a challenge.

A study of methods can offer suggestions for those drawn to the potential of uncovering this rich depth of knowledge, specifically about you. The first thing most books will say is to form an intention to remember and to put a journal and pen right next to your bed so that when you first wake you can write down immediately what happened. The issue I've always had is if you have a partner sharing your space, you don't want to blast them with the light it takes to write things down. Recording dreams becomes a procedural issue. One way to get around that is to leave a dream journal in the bathroom before you go to sleep. Then, when you wake up, repeat a few key words from your dream before you even open your eyes. Keep repeating them as you walk to the bathroom and then write out any other impressions that come. This helps with remembering in the morning. I use a night light for this process because I'm very sensitive to light and don't want to activate myself and have trouble falling back to sleep.

Over the years I have accumulated a dream journal with more than 200,000 words. Currently I use the app I described called *Dreams* which allows you to track your sleep, add in your dreams, and tag as you would a blog. In this way, you can look at dreams by symbols. The symbols will teach you much about yourself and your relationships. Remember how I told you about my *mermaid-ness*, as my husband calls it? You may guess that my main symbol is water, with a whopping 15 appearances over the past month. I can look at the reasons for that, and those aren't so easily determined by a dream dictionary which would call water "emotion" as it is for me perceiving that, depending on the type of water, I need to pay attention to what's around. The reason to place value on your dreams and study your symbols is that while you are sleeping, your ego is on break, and you can learn from an unedited subconscious about the Truth of what is really going on.

This moves into a different area when we get to nightmares and night terrors. While I've heard dream experts say the nightmares are there to help you, I've never actually seen dream workers successfully help people in this area. Instead, I've seen people suffer so deeply from night terrors, they don't want to sleep. That lack of sleep aggravates the night terrors and creates a vicious circle. It is currently believed also that night terrors are an indicator of early onset bipolar disorder, which points to the intersection of illness and a spiritual awakening. Which is which?

Light Lift 11: Shadow Work

Shadow work is tricky and absolutely necessary to get to your own brightest self. You don't want to sink down in the muck for long periods, but you don't want to spiritually bypass with thinking everything is just butterflies and unicorns. It's important to give everybody a seat at the table. If you don't know the term, I recommend Robert Ohotto's work in this area. He's a master at understanding that only by understanding your shadow archetypes, can you be fully lit.

CHAPTER TWELVE:

When Visions Get Scary

Were it not for shadows, there would be no beauty.

—Jun'ichiro Tanizaki, *In Praise of Shadows*

In many books I've read about spirituality and waking up, I've never seen the subject of mental illness addressed with more than a cursory mention. Yet in many spiritual circles, I've watched people go through a psychotic break while the people in the spiritual circle stand by, uncertain what to do. Unless the leader of that group has been through a very personal experience, they often struggle from a place of unknowing about how to help and address the situation with platitudes that offer the person little relief and, in some cases, make it worse.

Part of dreams, part of becoming conscious and moving into our next level of understanding as Souls, may involve visions, dreams at day, or dreams at night. However, when these visions or auditory sounds become frightening in any way, this has moved from a space of consciousness-opening to early signs of mental illness and should be addressed immediately with a professional, or better yet, a team of professionals. Or at least this is how it works in the United States.

Some people call this kundalini awakening. In more shamanic cultures, they look for the person with the visual and auditory hallucinations that appears to be in a psychotic break, throw them into the forest, and rejoice, for that person will be the next visionary for the tribe. It's a cause of celebration. Just as Sweden has an entirely different approach to The Covid than the U.S., cultures differ in the ways they look at dreams, visions, and mental illness.

This is all just philosophy that sits on the side of the road when you, or a child (sibling, parent, friend), begins having signs of a mental illness. In interviewing one man for our docuseries who had a break at 19 which later evolved into a schizophrenia diagnosis, he said that one of his early indicators that he could point to was an interest in metaphysical spaces and said that it had been known to be an indicator of early mental illness. As someone raised in traditional Baptist roots (not by my parents, but by a friend in town who took me with them and I like donuts, so I went), I became enamored with metaphysics as an alternative to the rigid thinking I found in organized religions. What I've seen more often in mental illness is rigid religiosity. For example, in the church I went to with my friend when I was young, my pastor would call my mom and tell her I was going to hell when I missed Sunday school. Metaphysics never told me that. In fact, metaphysics encouraged me to be a seeker and explore beyond the physical.

In Max Fagerquist's AP European History class in high school, we all sat in a circle on the first day and the teacher said, while tossing an oversized mint around his mouth: "Epistemology: why are you here?" Those were his first words. Imagine if every class began that way, encouraging independent thinking. That, I thought, was important to look at and answer, not because tribal thinking would tell me so, but because I needed to answer that for myself. Looking at the world from a non-western perspective was something I later became interested in and learned from by piecing all thoughts back together.

That's some solid years of interest in metaphysics, and I never had early symptoms of a mental illness or had a psychotic break. I wondered why our interviewee said that or where he'd heard that metaphysical thinking was an early sign of mental illness. I wondered if this could be the root of the problem in spiritual circles, a fear of those two circles overlapping in a Venn Diagram. I still don't know the answer, but I've learned I have a lot more questions about why there is this gray area that has to be one way or the other. Over the next few years in spiritual settings, I would see several people move from a metaphysical (or rigidly religious) framework where they appeared to be having an awakening that quickly morphed into a psychotic break with scary visions and dreams. Psilocybin was sometimes involved, or plant medicine (Ayahuasca), but not always.

Honestly, I think this means just as The Covid can affect anyone, so can mental illness. They are both the great equalizers. They both are great hiders, some peeking out and others hiding in dark corners. I believe we are all just one trigger away from a mental illness, or one exposure away from a pandemic. In both cases, when it happens for whatever reason, we need to track it early, put a plan in place that works for the unique being affected, gather resources and a "turn-around team," and make a move. The earlier the tracking of all that, the better the person can address what is happening in a healthy, educated way, and move through their journey in more of a balanced, peaceful place.

As my life purpose centers around bringing the sunshine to people and making their journeys less painful, my last 10 years have been dedicated to a vision of getting resources in the hands of teachers, parents, and the students themselves about mental-health tools to use in the pre-addiction phase, which gets younger and younger. Over this decade, I have seen so many more conversations about early intervention that make me happy and hopeful. I also see a huge increase in the problem.

We still have a long way to go, but yesterday something major happened: a joining of the traditional mental-health structure making a deal with the less traditional route. The Los Angeles Department of Mental Health signed a deal with Headspace, the meditation app. This is a recognition and acknowledgement that there are many paths to healing, as individual as the unique individuals themselves, and that meditation has been invited to the party. I remain hopeful, and think we are moving in the right direction.

Light Lift 12 – Energy Swipe

Stand with both feet on the ground. Reach your left hand to your right shoulder and swipe at a diagonal down the front of your body. Now reach your right hand to your left shoulder and swipe down the front of your body. Repeat three times on each side. Add this to your morning ritual and see what happens.

CHAPTER THIRTEEN:

Meditation Medication

A quiet mind is able to hear intuition over fear.

—Anonymous

For years, the Transcendental Meditation (TM) community, which trains people to meditate in a specific way, has shared story after story of how people meditating in a space can change everything happening around that space. It can stop wars, for example. There have been truckloads of scientific research that meditation reduces stress, increases health in all the bodies (physical, mental, emotional, spiritual), and can raise the happiness factors in people's lives. This applies to people of all ages all around the world. It's free, though some do make lots of money from teaching it, and this makes it available in many different shapes and forms.

I have been using meditation and guided visualization in my teaching, both of children and adults, for as long as I can remember. Both my children had their different kinds of restless energy and with my older, storytelling worked best. For my younger, meditation and guided visualization was very effective at bedtime. I noticed that the stress difference was tangible before and after. As my younger child got older, we trained together in TM, and during college this helped with anxiety, tremendously. Additionally, after a particularly trying semester, he found a music therapist near his school who did beautiful visualizations and brought him out of stress response almost immediately, which is really the key. I keep thinking how valuable Amy, the music therapist, would be right now to all the children and teens struggling with the changes that have come from The Covid and how they would find a whole new coping mechanism when the world starts up again and gets noisy.

Meditation, then, is quickly becoming recognized in the West as a practice to pack in your toolbox to help you really get to know you. It can be as easy or as complicated as you make it. With TM, you are given a mantra that only you and your teacher know, and you just repeat that silently, 20 minutes per session, two sessions per day. Honestly, I rarely make the second session, but when I do it's like working out twice. The effects are cumulative. It's not about dancing with your perfectionism. It's about finding that sacred space between breaths, that space where you are just you. The TM training is actually a four-day process, but it's a very good option for many and seems to have grabbed the attention of the Hollywood crowd.

Know, however, that TM isn't the only type of meditation that can help you. As many meditators that exist in the world, there are ways to meditate. If you like guided, there are about 1,000 apps where you can find guided meditations for free. For example, UCLA recently told me about their app after I took a mindfulness therapy class (free online—Go Bruins!) and on that app there are meditations of all lengths and types.

My daily favorite, which I love even more than my silent TM, is to listen to James Twyman's *Moses Code* in the background for 20 minutes and silently repeat "I am grateful I am" over and over. The story I've heard is that Twyman chose all the notes of the Universe so you can hear God speak when it plays. I don't know if that's true, but it feels like it to me. I feel a connection to all things when I sit with that and my Labrador Retriever Kai seems to, too. It's one of our favorite times of day. When my husband and I travel, it's our go-to upon waking.

It does not just happen though, this meditation gig. It works only if you work it. And I've noticed an inherent resistance that pushes back at the beginning of getting a practice going. Still, it's important, and all you have to do is sit. Build up slowly. Start at two minutes. Go to three. Keep going until you hit twenty minutes.

I will tell you a story. I have so many on this topic. My friend, Janelle (not her real name), was suffering. She'd reached this part of her life in her 60's where she just didn't know if it was worth going on. She never said the word "suicide," but I could tell she was leaning in that direction. We talked about meditation. She had a strict religious background, and she wasn't sure meditation was okay. I assured her it was. She began sitting each day. Then I lost track, until about six months later she wrote me a letter and said she had built a practice consisting of two 20-minute sessions each day and was a completely different person with a sense of hope about her. Her outside life was the same – it was she who had changed. How? Just by sitting on her butt and breathing twice a day.

Meditation can be the best medication of all.

Light Lift 13 – Download Calm

Here you can meditate for seven days with LeBron James, follow a guided mindfulness meditation or just find some music to sit and listen to for your practice. There are categories for beginners, anxiety, sleep, stress, self-care, inner peace, work, focus, emotions, less guidance, relationships, personal growth,kids and so on. There are both free and paid levels. Just explore. There are about a thousand apps out there. You can get lost down the rabbit hole. Just remember, though, that you don't need any of it. Sitting in a place, closing your eyes, and repeating, "in and out" with each breath works just find. More than anything, you do you, and find your Zen within.

CHAPTER FOURTEEN:

Speaking of Medication

Wherever the art of medicine is loved,
there is also a love of humanity.

—Hippocrates

I've noticed, specifically in spiritual circles, that there are certain notions about things. One of those things is judgments about medication. In my experience, I have seen medication save lives, offering tremendous relief for a person drowning in pain. I have also seen a resistance to medication for a variety of reasons, and side-effects that are difficult to live with. I've seen them both under- and over-prescribed. I've listened to arguments for and against. In some circles, I've seen people shamed and made to feel guilty if they take medications. These absolute views are extremely dangerous.

As we are all unique, each situation is going to be different. Just because medication may work for one person doesn't mean it is going to work for everyone. And just because it doesn't work for someone, doesn't mean it's bad for everyone else. If each of us is so unique and different, which we are, how can vaccinations be bad for everyone or good for everyone? How can medications (of any type) be bad for everyone or good for everyone? This all-or-nothing tribal thinking is where people get locked into group-thought forms, herd mentality, and can no longer think original thoughts for themselves. We need to stop that.

It's what The Covid is teaching us. As soon as we see what it is, it morphs into another mutation. We want to track our own mutations as we move through these experiences. We are constantly evolving, and as we wake up to ourselves, our needs change. We require different foods to fuel our body, and each body requires different things. A current shortage of seeds also means people will be fueled with more nutritious things they have grown. Have you ever tasted a sprout you have grown instead of one that comes from your local grocer? Worlds apart. You can feel the nutritious punch in just a pinch. I dare you to try it. This assist to our physical bodies will help the rest of us feel happier and healthier.

Still, each person is different. Getting to know your body, what makes it thrive and what makes it dive, is the most important thing. We need to apply this to each body: physical, mental, emotional, spiritual. Mind. Body. Spirit. Emotions. Feel into them. Surrender.

Light Lift 14 – Get to Know Your Guidance Team

Each person has a guidance team whether they believe it or not. Religions often tell us who our guidance team is comprised of and use guilt and shame to keep us from digging any further, least we offend their mandate. And yet, we still have a guidance team always standing by to help. When you ask to know them, they will appear, often in the ways you can best receive.

Close your eyes. Imagine you are in a place that brings you deep peace. Recreate the space in your imagination. Is there water nearby? Plants? What's the temperature? What do you hear? Feel? Smell? When you have created your perfect space in your mind, ask one of your guides to come forward. Ask questions and get to know it like a new friend. Visit often. Interact. You are never alone, and they are so eager to help you.

CHAPTER FIFTEEN:

The Grudges We Hold, Hold Us

When you hold a grudge, you want someone else's sorrow to reflect your level of hurt, but the two rarely meet.

—Steve Maraboli

With The Covid in full drama as I write this, we witness numerous opportunities for our global family to hold collective grudges. The news will tell us all about it. Individually, in houses around the world, each of us is having to not only face themselves up close, but also those they share space with. As tensions rise, and we each dive into coping mechanisms, we see each other in completely new ways, and not always for the better, as illustrated in that Wuhan divorce spike I mentioned earlier. The fact that *Tiger King* with all its mayhem and drama became the most popular Netflix show at the start of The Covid suggests that collectively we are searching for those with just a little more mess than we have.

We can help ourselves get clearer about where we can shine once we clear out the smoke. It's a good time to look at the grudges each of us may secretly hold. Have you ever tried to list each and every person in your life who has wronged you? I have done this on a number of occasions through different classes and during my practitioner training. I am always exhausted by my list. When you have to go back and explain all the reasons why each person wronged you and how, the task can feel overwhelming. If just listing all those names, or situations, or politicians, or you-name-it takes so much energy, imagine what we could do when it all washes down the drain. (I literally do that with this list. Wash the ink off the page and down the drain.) This lifts about 20 pounds I didn't know I was carrying off my shoulders.

When we give someone else the gift of forgiveness in this way, we give this gift to ourselves. We do not forgive someone else for their sake; we do it for our own. Carrying those grudges around is just too heavy. And we can't secretly carry them and say we don't. This causes even more dullness to our shine. Even as I type this, I can access in my mind the hardest ones to forgive. Those are the ones who hurt my children, and anyone else's children. And still, holding on to these grudges just holds me down, keeps me from fully realizing who I am at my core: a spiritual being full of light living in a physical body, connected to all the other spiritual beings full of light living in their physical bodies. This is you. We see separate bodies so we forget this, but when we look at this unprecedented time in our history, we can see more clearly than ever just how connected we are. We are we.

But how do we do this forgiveness thing when we have so much pain and anger? Forgiving is not for the other person; forgiving is for you. Forgiving does not mean you have to reconnect with the other person or talk to them or agree with what they did. The pain is a clear guidance that can navigate you to your peace place when you let it. The stronger the pain, the more this grudge shackles you; hardly ever the other. To release those shackles, I am reminded of the great Hawaiian wisdom that is spot-on when it comes to forgiveness practice: Ho'oponopono.

In this easy-to-say, hard-to-mean, spirit-transforming practice you put a thing or a person in front of your mind who has wronged you in some way, who sets off an emotional charge in you. Picture them there. You then say these words, known as the Ho'oponopono Prayer:

> I Love You
> I Am Sorry
> Please Forgive Me
> Thank you

You repeat this until you mean it. Fake it 'til you make it, because some are harder to do than others. What I can promise is that as soon as it takes, there is a weight lifted that is palpable. A peace waits there for you. You realize how heavy holding the thing was. Boundaries don't require any further movement if none is desired. Forgiving is for you, to make you happier, to make you lighter, to make you shine brighter. Let go of those grudges so they let go of you.

Light Lift 15 – Unchain Your Chains

Start with something small, like that person who cut you off in traffic. On the scale from 1-10, how angry are you? Note the number. Say the prayer. Repeat it again and again. On a scale from 1-10, how angry are you? Rinse, lather, repeat until you get to 0. Then make your list, and practice your forgiveness muscles, saving the heaviest weights for when your muscles are strong. Oh, the places you'll go.

CHAPTER SIXTEEN:

The Gratitude Game Changer

I am grateful I am.

—My daily meditation mantra

Just think. What if we could make gratitude go viral? What if gratitude became the next pandemic? What kind of different world would we be living in?

At Yale University, Professor Laurie Santos teaches a popular class called the *Science of Well-Being*. In this class, she gives numerous scientific studies that show people who make a practice of gratitude are happier. People who make a habit of telling other people they are grateful, writing it down, becoming conscious of the things they are grateful for and otherwise breathing life into specific gratitude, experience much joy and happiness. In fact, for the greatest boost of all, says Santos, write a gratitude letter and read it out loud to someone. For the best hit, you want to write this out long hand, meet them in person, and read it to them. Who doesn't want to be that person on the receiving end of that letter? Still, this is not for the person receiving, but rather for you. Studies say this gratitude high lingers for weeks. The beauty is that the person to whom you are reading will benefit so much by knowing your true feelings.

In Santos' class, as part of the *rewirements* you are to write down *gratitudes* in the app each day. A marked difference can be felt when you are actually writing these down vs. just thinking about an attitude of gratitude. It's a clear argument for daily gratitude journals or emailing a gratitude list of three things to a friend each day, which adds another level of accountability. I often see this done during the month of December on social media but making this a daily thing can bring you into full shine.

I'm reminded of a story of my younger son when he was voicing his list of the many things that were wrong at the time. After he was finished venting, which is an important part of the process, we asked him, on a 30-minute car ride back to the town where we lived, to shift his perspective. We asked him to focus on all the things he was grateful for, which he said would be easy because "he was the most grateful person he knew." We asked him to prove it by listing out in a stream of consciousness thread each gratitude that entered his mind without repeating himself. The entire ride home he looked out the window and offered one gratitude after another with all of us laughing in the end about how many things he came up with and how he'd started in such a cantankerous headspace. The transformation was joyful for all of us. This same son recently responded to a gratitude letter I wrote him with gratitude back, not only for the things I wrote to him, but also with a heart opening "Mom, I really see how you are living in the world from a place of gratitude, and that's awesome."

The Universe loves a grateful Soul and really does offer an attitude of "oh you think that was good, wait until you see what I have next!" Showing gratitude greases that wheel in a way nothing else can. Nothing.

Just know this: I'm grateful for you, you beautiful Soul. There is nobody like you.

Light Lift 16 – Gratitude Begins With You

Try writing a different kind of gratitude letter. This one you will write to yourself. Write to yourself in the tone you would write to your best friend. List all the things about you that you are grateful for and don't leave anything out. Pretend you are on that 30-minute car ride and don't stop until you're home and pulling in the garage.

CHAPTER SEVENTEEN:

In-Tuition: Invest in Deep Knowing

There is a voice that doesn't use words.

—Rumi

Intuition. It's just not a construct that we know how to integrate in Western society. Even in spiritual circles, depending on the circle, the word can rub people the wrong way. Why?

Intuition lives in all of us. We all have psychic abilities. It's long been called a feminine attribute, but intuition is not a gender thing. We need to let that go. This great resource we have is one that can save our lives. It will also transform our world if we as individuals learn to embrace its value, and as a collective, actively develop it.

Like dreams, the first step toward developing intuition is to trust that you can. You can! In cultures where this is cultivated it's fascinating to see how powerful intuition can be. In many cultures around the globe, intuition is actually taught in early-childhood education. This is not true in the West, though Native American cultures seem to nurture it better than the mainstream. For now, intuition is a topic taught by metaphysical teachers in books and online courses. It can be developed by independent study, both with children and adults, and children actually have fewer blocks to this concept because generally they are more open-minded. The secret is to open to the possibility and quiet your mind. This leads back to meditation as the perfect portal for mind-quieting. A key part of intuition is learning to trust yourself, as well as keeping cumulative track of your own intuitions and how they play out. The more you do this, the sharper it becomes.

Start to look at the world with a keen eye. Become an intuition detective. Notice the subtle reactions in your own body as somebody says something. You will feel it somatically and you will start to notice patterns, just as you do with your dream symbols. Your body will help guide you. You know that saying "I feel it in my gut?" Sometimes, it's in your chest. Sometimes, in your shoulders. Just shifting your attention to where you feel this in your body will help you learn. Your whole body will go online and understand you are paying attention. It will help you out.

Intuition can transform your world. Enter into your intuition with curiosity, a beginner's mind wanting to learn. Love yourself. Be graceful, letting your perfectionist take a nap while you play. And then play! Play with different tools. One time when we were on the Big Island in a place called Hawi we walked into what I thought was a jewelry shop but was actually a crystal shop. It was one of the first crystal shops I had ever walked in. As we stepped inside, I couldn't move. The room started spinning and I felt like I was going to fall over. The woman at the counter came over to check on me. I told her what was going on and that I wasn't sure what it was. She said, "Oh, that's easy. You're just really sensitive to energy." She handed me a black tourmaline and the whole vibe changed. To this day, if I walk into a crystal shop, I'll go pick up a black tourmaline first and carry it around with me, thank it for its stabilizing force, and hand it back at the counter.

I'm now a huge proponent of these crystal tools and use them to incubate dreams, deepen meditation, give to friends, and aid in past-life regression and future-life progression (for myself and others). They increase intuition and smooth the edges on dreams. They deepen meditation. As we all carry energy, so do they, and perhaps this is why. I try not to get too hung up on the why. I'm more interested in what works.

There is an abundant supply of tools out there, courses to take, books to read, workshops to explore to increase intuition if this is something that appeals to you, as it does to me. In the meantime, become a student of your own reactions in your body to things. That will teach you so much.

Don't expect cheerleaders. I have yet to find many of those in my life who encourage me to trust my intuition and recognize how strong it's become over the years. The few I have are priceless gems. Do expect critics and doubters. I have plenty of those. Don't let them dim you down. Remember, their skepticism is about them, not about you. Be your own cheerleader. Keep practicing and know that by developing your intuition, you're making the world a better place.

Light Lift 17: Somatic Scan

Close your eyes. Breathe deeply in and out. Focus your attention on your feet first and begin scanning your entire body while continuing to breathe. Go slow. Scan each toe, your foot, your ankle, your calves, your thighs, your buttocks, your genitalia, your stomach, chest, arms, shoulders, neck, face, and head all the way up to your hair follicles. Now, go back down. Do this when you're relaxed and when you're stressed. Pay attention to the different ways your body talks to you. It has so much to say and can be such a great partner in developing intuition.

CHAPTER EIGHTEEN:

Be Like Water

Nothing is softer or more flexible than water,
yet nothing can resist it.

—Lao Tzu

I often wondered if Anthony loved water for the same reasons I did; if he saw the same sacred lessons that it has to teach us. What drew him there?

Before I could walk, I swam. Born a spring baby in a land where summers were 115 degrees of sweltering heat and living with just a swamp cooler that didn't work very well in extreme heat, I spent the entire summers, sun-up to sun-down, in the swimming pool. My white blonde hair was green June through August. I remember that pool, just an above-ground thing with a deck surrounding it, where I'd build mermaid caves with floats and pretend I was living in an underwater kingdom. My friend

Laurie would come over and we would lie on floats and talk for hours and just be.

As I got older, I started creek floating, spending the entire day bobbing from one end of the creek on an inner tube to the other where a car would be parked. This journey would take the entire day, bodies burnt from the relentless sun, asses frozen from winter's snow melt. I would learn that while flowing down the creek, you need to lie very flat underneath hot irrigation pipes that crossed over or you would get knocked in the head, and when white water came, your attention needed to be at its best. These were good metaphors for life.

The first time I saw the ocean, I understood the vast power of water. It was incredible. This body of water that demanded respect had a whole different world beneath it, and never disappointed, with its steady in-and-out, in-and-out of waves kissing the shore.

My dad used to say, "Just go with the flow, JR." I hated it when he said that because it meant I wasn't doing it. I wanted to be a good girl, but I wasn't.

In Sedona, a guide showed me a river and he said, "You see how that bright yellow leaf floats down the river? You see how it bobs and weaves around the rocks? You are that leaf, that leaf that flows down the river."

I wanted to tell him, "No. I am the river."

When we get in *flow*, a concept that has been taken on by Michael Csikszentmihalyi and explained in his book by the same title, we lose time. When we lose time, we are floating in our passion, finding our bliss, as Joseph Campbell called it, doing that thing that is most us, that highlights our unique selves. Flow, then, is yet another tool we find as we move like the river, gliding around rocks and carrying others so they don't hit hot irrigation pipes. As water fills a space and holds us, we fill a space and hold ourselves and others high. As the ocean shows up for the sand over and over again, we show up for ourselves, knowing that as we stay in flow, tools will come, tools that we need to figure out for our unique selves. As the water cools us off under a hot sun, and allows for imaginal kingdoms to be built, we show gratitude by engaging with it consciously, water to water, for this is what we are. Without water, there is no life.

"Go with the flow, JR."

These words are now ones I hold close to my heart. I remember the baby dolphin's leaf game and the joy of play. I remember the leaf floating, dodging obstacles, and thinking of myself as both the leaf and the river. I remember not to force my way upstream but to look at the flow pattern and drop into that. Float. Flow. Not chasing, for chasing is hard to do in the water. Choose to let the water carry you, to hold you, to lift you up, and in so doing, you lift the world. Be like water.

Light Lift 18: Be the Sea

Get some Epsom Salt. Pour it in the bathtub. Light a candle. Turn off the lights. Turn on Deuter's "Reiki Hands of Love." Submerge. Close your eyes. Breathe. Repeat. Repeat. Repeat.

CHAPTER NINETEEN:

Past, Present, Future You

Take pride in how far you've come and have faith in how far you can go. But don't forget to enjoy the journey.

—Michael Josephson

One of the best tools I've found to understanding your You-nique shine is by looking at themes that run through your past, present, and future lives. Don't miss out on playing this game, even if you don't believe that a Soul moves through multiple lifetimes. Just imagine what you would write if you were to make up a story of you in a past life. Be like the dolphin with the leaf game and just play. Don't lock yourself down by getting too serious about it. You can't do this wrong.

If you had a past life, what might it be? What would you wear? Where would you live? What would your job be? What would you eat? Would you have any of the same talents that you have in this life? Let your imagination take you without risk to a place where that might be.

Repeat the same process for a future life. Where would you live? Who would you love? Are you alone or with someone else? What do you eat? What do you wear? Do you have any of the same talents you have in this life?

When I lead a past-life regression, future-life progression session, or in-between session (my favorite!) it generally takes two hours so I don't mean to imply this will happen in the amount of space it took to write that. It will take longer, and you should give yourself time and space. When I first became interested in this tool about 15 years ago, I was in Boynton Canyon (Sedona, Arizona) again at Enchantment Resort which was the place I mentioned we were when The Covid came to town and again over the Solstice for our 23rd wedding anniversary. In that early visit, I had signed up for an experience at the spa that led me to Dr. Brian Weiss's work. Dr. Weiss was a Western psychiatrist who couldn't help his patient with anxiety for two years, so finally, behind closed doors so his peers didn't think he was a freak, hypnotized his patient back to when the anxiety started, and she went back two-thousand years. He then decided, because he cared about helping his clients and doing what was best for them, that he needed to look into regression as a tool. A leading expert in the field, his work and bravery – his willingness to be an original thinker and transcend the herd – inspired me so much I went back to Sedona some years later to become certified as a regression therapist myself.

It's a powerful tool not only to better understand who you are in this lifetime, but who you are in the process of becoming. It's not a place to get lost, but rather a place to find information on how to best find happiness and shine in this lifetime.

Light Charge #19: Picture This

Take a pad and a pencil and go outside. Fold the page in half vertically and horizontally to create 4 frames or draw a cross, so you have four squares. Pick a scene. In the first quarter, draw it. Do not judge yourself or hold attachment to your artistic ability. It doesn't matter. Just study a tree, or a flower, and draw it. In the second frame across from it, imagine what was there 100 years ago. Draw it. In the third frame, below the first one, imagine what will be there in 100 years. Draw it. In the last square, draw the scene in the present again. Look at them all and notice any similarities or differences.

CHAPTER TWENTY:

It's Always Been You

To be beautiful means to be yourself.
You don't need to be accepted by others.
You need to accept yourself.

—Thich Nhat Hanh

In the end, we are all here, snowflakes all, with our unique and beautiful designs as only we have. Imagine that. It's mindboggling, really. When I look at people, it's often so clear to me what their unique imprint is; and I want to show them. I want them to see for themselves. I think Anthony and I shared this in common. At that moment when I talked to his high-school friend, leaning over to hear her in the noise of the room and smelling her young daughter's newly shampooed hair as she held her, wanting to make all the right moves, I was struck by how we're all just doing the best we can with what we've gathered on our journeys. Babies raising babies. Trying to do our best, but often without role models. Trying to fill their holes, but not knowing where their next child's meal will come from. Through her tears came her words, barely audible, "He captured the beauty in everybody else, beauty they couldn't see for themselves. He captured my beauty." Through my tears, I nodded. I thought about his comment to me on Mother's Day, noticing that I was good at the thing I most cared about more than anything else in the world. He didn't even know why he noticed it, he'd said. At that point, he was couch surfing or living on the street, lost in his addiction, the mask for his untreated mental-health holes, and he took the time to show me my beauty in a way that was and still is so meaningful. The words she said next, this young momma, stick with me. When I choked out my words enough to ask if he saw any of his own beauty that we saw, she said, "No. He never got the chance." Our foreheads touched, and tears streamed down our cheeks.

My vision is that you will look deeply within yourself right now and see your beauty. I see it and I love you. Go to your mirror like Louise Hay used to teach in her mirror work and say, "I love you. I really, really love you." No, really. Do it. No excuses. Face it, you're worth it.

But not only are you worth it, your world needs the You-nique you that only you can give. We're all waiting. Find the holes in your trust and fill them. Be brave. Dream it. Sit with it. Listen to the voice behind the voice. Watch early signs of all things for clues. Let go of tribal thinking and be the original you are.

Find your bliss and follow it, as it will lead you to your joy and help you see what Spirit wants to create through you. You can do it. There are others out there floundering in silence who need that fierceness you have down deep. Find guidance from unlikely teachers, even a pandemic. Stay curious. Keep learning just to learn. Be grateful. Forgive everyone, and mostly yourself.

Follow the signs, the synchronicities, as they will lay out the path you are meant to follow. Breathe in the moment, be here now, and you will find in the backyard of your own Soul, the same sacred space we chase in the oceans of the Pacific, flying in the skies, walking down the Camino, or soaking up the hot springs at Esalen.

Meet yourself where you are. As you tread water and giggle, look around: the sacred spaces are chasing you. Here come the dolphins. They see you shine.

Made in the USA
Monee, IL
21 December 2020